THE RAFT

The RAFT

ROBERT TRUMBULL

*With a foreword and afterword
by John M. Waters, Captain, USCG (Ret.)*

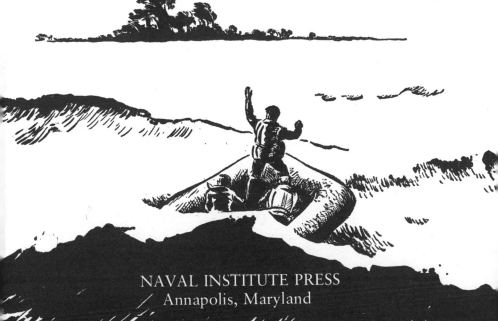

NAVAL INSTITUTE PRESS
Annapolis, Maryland

© 1942 by Henry Holt and Company, Inc.
Foreword and afterword © 1992
by the United States Naval Institute
Annapolis, Maryland

Library of Congress Cataloging-in-Publication
Data

Trumbull, Robert
    The raft / Robert Trumbull : with a foreword and afterword by
John M. Waters.
        p.   cm.
    ISBN 1-55750-827-5
    1. World War, 1939–1945—Aerial operations, American.   2.
Survival after airplane accidents, shipwrecks, etc.   3. Shipwrecks—
Pacific Ocean.   I. Title.
D790.T78   1992
940.54'8173—dc20   91-25085

Printed in the United States of America on acid-free paper ∞

11   10   09   08   07   06   11   10   9   8   7   6

Map by William Clipson

FOREWORD

To truly appreciate the epic tale of survival told in *The Raft,* one must first look at the setting in which it occurred, which the original edition, published in 1942, could not reveal because of wartime secrecy rules.

Following the Japanese attack on Pearl Harbor on 7 December 1941, America and its Allies were thrown on the defensive around the world. Japanese forces streamed into the Philippines, Malaya, Indonesia, and the islands of the Central and Southwest Pacific in a series of uninterrupted victories, while in the Atlantic rampaging U-boats threatened to close down the East Coast ports of the United States. With much of its battleship strength smashed at Pearl Harbor, and little likelihood of British help following the sinking of the *Prince of Wales* and *Repulse* in the Gulf of Siam, the Pacific Fleet had only three carriers—the *Enterprise, Saratoga,* and *Lexington*—and their supporting cruisers and destroyers to protect Hawaii from the mighty Japanese Combined Fleet. Before Christmas, the Pacific Fleet aborted an attempt to reinforce the hard-pressed garrison at Wake Island because the top command realized that waiting Japanese forces could be in a position to inflict crippling losses on the carriers. To the men of the fleet, desperate to help their brothers on Wake, the strategic picture was not so clear, and morale dropped amid bitter grumbling when the relief attempt was canceled.

Safeguarding the sea lines of communication to Australia through the Allied islands of Samoa and New Caledonia was the first priority. In early January a fast troop convoy carrying the 2nd Marine Brigade sailed from San Diego to reinforce the defenses of Samoa. The convoy's escort was the newly formed Task Force 17, with Rear Admiral Frank Jack Fletcher flying his flag in the *Yorktown*, freshly arrived from the Atlantic Fleet.

At the same time, Admiral Ernest J. King, Commander in Chief, U.S. Fleet, urged the new Commander in Chief, Pacific Fleet, Admiral Chester W. Nimitz, to take "some aggressive action for effect on general morale," a move Nimitz was already planning. On 8 January 1942 Nimitz ordered Vice Admiral William F. "Bull" Halsey in the *Enterprise* to sortie with Task Force 8 (one carrier, three cruisers, and seven destroyers), join with Fletcher's Task Force 17, and after delivery of the troop convoy to Samoa, strike Japanese installations in the Marshalls and Gilberts at the beginning of February. It was to be the first counterattack of the war.

Embarked on the *Enterprise* was Carrier Air Group Six, and its torpedo-bomber squadron was VT-6 (Torpedo Six), which listed among its members Harold F. Dixon, Anthony

J. Pastula, and Gene D. Aldrich, three men only casually acquainted, who were soon to face a terrifying ordeal of forced togetherness. Task Force 8 crossed the equator near Howland Island, where Amelia Earhart had disappeared less than five years before, but the ships observed none of the traditional line-crossing ceremonies because of the serious war situation and the men's general disgruntlement. On 16 January 1942 aircraft from the *Enterprise* continued their aggressive patrolling for Japanese submarines believed in the area. The carrier *Saratoga* had been torpedoed northwest of Oahu the previous week and had limped back to Pearl Harbor, screened by the rest of Task Force 14. The *Lexington* and Task Force 11, badly in need of replenishment, followed the *Saratoga* into Pearl. With Task Force 17 guarding the vital troop convoy, Halsey's *Enterprise* was for the moment the Navy's only carrier available for immediate use, and nothing short of an all-out disaster would interfere with her mission, as Dixon, Pastula, and Aldrich would soon discover.

That morning, one of the *Enterprise*'s torpedo-bombers crashed on landing, mortally wounding a chief petty officer operating the arresting gear. Later, two sailors died in accidents on other ships of the force. By the time Dixon, Pastula, and Aldrich manned TBD Devastator aircraft 6-T-6—a low-wing, single-engine torpedo-bomber made by Douglas—for the afternoon antisubmarine patrol, it had not been a good day.

All three of the crew members were petty officers, Dixon being a chief aviation machinist's mate. He was also a des-

ignated Naval Aviation Pilot (NAP). Officer pilots were des-
ignated Naval Aviators (NAs), though both groups had the
same aviation training and wore identical gold wings. The
Navy had started training enlisted men as pilots in the First
World War and continued doing so except for the years 1931–
35, when none were trained because of a lack of funds. In
1926 Congress dictated that the number of enlisted pilots
could not exceed 30 percent of the number of officer pilots,
and the following year Fighting Squadron VF-2 was set up
to test the feasibility of mixed NA-NAP manning. At the
outbreak of war VF-2 had six NAs and sixteen NAPs, and a
record of performance and readiness unsurpassed in the fleet.
The NAPs ranked from chief down to second class. Service-
wide, 13 percent of all pilots in the Navy, Coast Guard, and
Marine Corps were enlisted, and the practice was common
in other nations and services, though not in the Army Air
Corps. The enlisted pilots quickly established a fine combat
record, and most were later commissioned. The NAP desig-
nator was abolished in the postwar sea services, though the
last of the enlisted pilots did not retire until the 1970s.

Chief Dixon, at forty-one a seasoned Navy veteran with
twenty-two years of service, was considerably older than his
two crewmen. Pastula, a twenty-four-year-old aviation ordnanceman second class, was the bomber in the mid-cockpit
seat; Aldrich, twenty-two, an aviation radioman third class,
was the radioman and rear-seat gunner. The three had never
flown together as a team and were only casually acquainted.
Dixon recounts the story of their last flight and subsequent

adventures in the pages that follow, but he leaves the reader with some troubling questions.

First, how did they become lost on this relatively short flight? Anyone who has ever flown over water has at some time been lost, but most resolve their dilemma and fly home. Aerial navigation by tactical aircraft was rather primitive at the time, mostly dead reckoning—calculating position by the courses steered, indicated air speed, and time on each leg. Pilots had to make allowances and corrections for sometimes unreliable magnetic compasses, but changing winds were the biggest sources of error. To calculate the wind, a pilot used an E6B navigation plotter, entering wind-drift readings taken on various headings with a drift indicator instrument, or simply eyeballed the surface and estimated the wind. Both methods could be either highly accurate or badly in error, depending on the expertise of the observer. On most flights, proper preflight planning and execution brought the plane back within sight of the carrier or near enough (forty miles) to pick up the ship's YE radio beacon transmitter and home in with the aircraft's ZB receiver. The YE beacon was a short-range, highly directional radio that transmitted a different alphabet letter in Morse code for each fifteen-degree sector. The pilot had merely to listen, identify the sector in which he was flying, and fly inbound on the mid-sector heading to reach the carrier. The ship changed the sector alignments daily to prevent enemy aircraft from homing in on the signal.

Early in the war the *Enterprise* had the CXAM radar, a primitive type installed in 1941. It had a maximum range of perhaps 80 miles on large, high-flying formations, and as little as 20–30 miles on single aircraft. Because few of the aircraft were then equipped with IFF (Identification Friend or Foe) transponders, there was some confusion as to an individual aircraft's identity in a crowded sky. A troubled pilot could not expect the instant radar steers that became commonplace later in the war with the advent of better equipment, and of course any radar help required ship-to-plane radio contact.

Attack aircraft at the time carried a short-range voice radio (VHF), good for perhaps fifty miles at five thousand feet, and a medium-frequency (MF) Morse code set, operated by the rear-seat radioman, that was capable of long-range communications. The MF set was notoriously unreliable because of atmospheric noise and dead spots, as well as circuit malfunctions that occurred frequently in the warm, moist, salty atmosphere. Consequently, pilots flying from carriers often found themselves without long-range communications.

What mistakes in navigation Dixon made that day may never be known. Plane 6-T-6 encountered another plane from the squadron when well out on its search leg, and one of them must have been out of its sector. Dixon, however, did not become concerned for some time afterward, even taking time to make practice bombing runs on a smoke float. En route to the carrier, Aldrich, the radioman, heard Japanese traffic on the MF radio and pulled out his transmitter plug to indicate to the pilot that he was observing radio silence on that channel.

When he did not sight the carrier as expected, Dixon called

on his short-range VHF radio, but he received no answer, nor any signal from the YE. Examining the matter after nearly fifty years, one must conclude that some errors in navigation probably occurred on the outbound leg, causing 6-T-6 to wander into another sector. As both the VHF voice and the YE homing beacon had been working early in the flight, it is most likely that the lost plane was more than fifty miles from the carrier and simply out of VHF range when Dixon attempted to establish contact during his return.

With fuel running low, Dixon decided to ditch while he still had power and daylight, and he reviewed with his crew what equipment to carry on leaving the plane. Then he made what all three men later described as a beautiful power-stall landing.

When the plane came to rest, the three men quickly passed the raft to Dixon, who had climbed out onto the wing. He encountered some difficulty with a malfunctioning inflation valve, and before he could inflate the raft, the plane suddenly sank beneath them, carrying most of the survival gear down with it. The loss is understandable—neither back-seat crewman was a proficient swimmer.

Though they had carried out their "abandon ship" promptly, the three were now in the water with no equipment other than the raft and life vests. When improved survival gear was later developed, much of it would be stowed within the raft to ensure it did not go down with the plane. But the three men of 6-T-6 would have to get by with what little they had salvaged. They realized the inadequacy of their supplies the very first morning when a search plane flew close by and the survivors had no means of signaling it.

The lack of a more thorough search is not remarkable. The task force had a far more compelling mission than looking for survivors of one downed plane and did not wait in the area. Although humanitarians may disapprove, combat commanders nearly always assign destruction of the enemy a higher priority than rescue of survivors when the two tasks conflict, and Dixon accepted this reality early on. Furthermore, one of the search planes ditched on the morning of the 17th, having run out of fuel, and Task Force 8 had to suspend flying in the afternoon to refuel its ships.

Finding themselves in a life raft in an empty ocean with very little gear, the men did not know where they were, nor what their prospects of survival were. The plane had gone down just south of the equator some 1,900 miles southwest of Hawaii. So their position was about 600 miles southeast of Tarawa and the Japanese-occupied Gilbert and Marshall Islands, but 700 miles northwest of American Samoa, from which a long chain of hundreds of islands, still in Allied hands, stretched 1,500 miles south and west through Fiji and New Caledonia. Furthermore, the survivors knew that Japanese submarines were operating in the area. Dixon, the leader and only qualified navigator of the three, determined to try and reach one of the American atolls. Though he attempted to guide the raft to the southwest, it finally landed on Puka Puka, a New Zealand–governed atoll in the Danger Islands, 346 miles northeast of Samoa and 423 miles from the ditching point, on 19 February. To get to Puka Puka, however, the raft had meandered on various courses for an estimated 1,200 miles. Though the men's efforts to navigate their craft had only a minor effect on the raft's movements, those efforts did afford the castaways some feeling of controlling their destiny and helped to sustain morale.

The story of the voyage, with few resources except courage and indomitable human spirit, is not only inspiring reading, but a tribute to the human species and its will to survive. The miraculous escapes, especially the passage over a killer reef and the reaching of safety only a day ahead of a typhoon, also suggest that Someone was looking over them!

JOHN M. WATERS
Captain, USCG (Ret.)

EQUATOR

GILBERT
ISLANDS

⊕ *Plane went down*

PHOENIX ISLANDS

South Pacific

ELLICE
ISLANDS

Raft came ashore

↓

Puka Puka
Nassau

DANGER ISLANDS

SAMOA ISLANDS

FIJI

JAPAN

Midway Is.

Marianas Is.

• Wake Is.

Caroline Is.

Marshall Is.

NEW
GUINEA

Gilbert Is.

Solomon Is.

Ellice Is.

AUSTRALIA

Fiji

PREFACE

. . . Bomber Pilot Harold Dixon was a man that Bligh would fancy.
                                   —TIME, March 23, 1942

CAPTAIN BLIGH would indeed have fancied Dixon. The famous Englishman, with his 17 men from the mutinied *Bounty*, accomplished a classic of the sea that men will never weary of telling. But for his 48-day voyage from Tofua, in the South Pacific, to Timor, Netherlands East Indies, a distance of 3,618 miles, he had a 23-foot boat. Dixon, Pastula, and Aldrich, to cover a thousand miles in 34 days, had an inflated rubber raft eight feet by four feet over-all. Captain Bligh had 32 pounds of pork, 150 pounds of bread, 28 gallons of water, six quarts of rum, six bottles of wine, a quadrant, a compass, and canvas. Dixon and his two companions had a pocketknife, a pair of pliers, an automatic pistol that soon became useless from corrosion, and a length of line. They had no food, no water, no instruments, no means of controlling their tiny fabric boat.

Dixon devised a series of ingenious makeshifts that enabled him to control his craft and chart his course. But the raft tipped over so easily in the heavy Pacific swells that in the end he and his two young sailors had nothing—not even a shred of clothing to protect them from the equatorial sun. Before they lost their clothes they were able to catch drinking water by soaking their rags when it rained, and wringing them into an oar pocket. They pulled their food from the air and the sea—a very little food, that was; not enough, as Dixon said, to make them one good meal.

It was no wonder, then, that they were given up for dead. But Dixon sailed that raft, made it go where he wanted it to go, and brought his men through.

When I saw them for the first time at Pearl Harbor, they looked like any three men of our navy such as I might meet on Waikiki Beach, or looking for an afternoon's amusement on Hotel Street. That was the wonder of the story to me: they *were* just three men who happened to have been assigned to take up a scout bomber from a carrier prowling the far South Pacific. When they got into that plane they barely knew each other by sight. They could have been any chief petty officer, any two sailors of their ratings. But they were men like these.

Dixon, the spokesman for the trio, came to my house at Waikiki for a week end, and we talked the best part of a night and a day. This book is the result.

I have tried to tell the story much as Dixon told it to me.

ROBERT TRUMBULL

Honolulu

CHAPTER · ONE

THE plane struck the surface of the sea with a sound like the slap of a giant hand on the water. A great splash of water instantly covered the glass in front of me, momentarily shutting out my vision. Two sharp bumps, and the plane settled quietly back on the long, slow swells. I had made a good landing.

As I rose from my seat in quick concern for Gene, Tony, the raft, and a multitude of things that competed for my attention in this crowded moment, I was conscious that the plane was bobbing gently up and down, but that at any second a wave might pull a wing, and we'd be gone. The sea that had looked so flat and solid from the air was now a reaching, greedy thing that shook its prey before devouring it.

I knew that our small three-man scout bomber would not float long. It is no great trick to set a land plane down on water, but these heavily armored war jobs are not intended to float. I had no idea of staying with it very long.

I jumped as quickly as I could onto the left wing to receive the raft from Tony Pastula, my bomber, and he was right there to hand it to me without an instant's delay. Gene Aldrich, my radioman and gunner, was raising himself from the rear cockpit and was busy with his gear. I was already trying to open the raft's gas valve, which seemed to stick.

Suddenly there was no airplane. The next thing I knew I was hanging in my life jacket, kicking the water.

The sinking of that plane was like a magician's trick. It was there, and then it was gone, and there was nothing left in our big, wet, darkening world but the three of us and a piece of rubber that was not yet a raft.

Of course the plane took with it everything the two boys in their well-disciplined haste had pulled together from emergency stores and equipment. I was soon to discover that what fight we were to make for our lives must depend upon the "junk" in our pockets, tools attached to the raft, which were so negligible in value as to be almost frivolous, and the uses we could make of the clothes upon our backs. All these things were to stand us well until they were wrested from our grasp, one by one, by the great unseeable enemy we fought, and then our only weapon was the mind, until this too began to go in the particular corrosion to which it is susceptible.

Finally I got the raft blown up, but the thing inflated itself upside down. Fortunately there was a handrail around it, of half-inch manila line. As soon as the raft expanded to its full size we had grabbed hold of this. I was at the bow, and struggled to twist the raft right side up, with the boys holding on so that we were fighting each other's weight as well as the clumsy vessel. After I struggled for fifteen or twenty minutes, with the sea banging me in the face and filling my mouth with salt water, I did get the raft turned over once. I can't remember for sure whether I tried to climb onto it, or not. The only thing I recall is that the raft flopped over, and I was mighty anxious to get on it.

The handrail ran along the side, and the boys, across from me, had a grip on it. The raft weighed only forty pounds, and their weight tipped it right over again on top of them. My work had been for nothing.

By this time we had been floundering and coughing in the water for quite a while, and were all exhausted. So then we calmed down and hung onto the handrail to rest.

It was quite dark now, but our eyes were becoming accustomed to it and we could see quite well, as anyone can after a few minutes in what at first seems to be pitch blackness.

Gene spoke first.

[3]

"There's a way to get this thing over," he said, still a little short of breath.

Those deliberate words, spoken in a slow Missouri drawl with no more or less concern than if he were laboring over a recalcitrant mowing machine on his father's farm, brought our problem back to matter-of-factness.

"We've got to stop and dope us out a scheme," I said. Tony chimed in.

"All right," he said, blowing sea water from his lips, "how about we take off our blouses, tie 'em together, tie one end to the line on one side of the boat, throw that up across the bottom of the boat, then we all go to the other side and pull, and see if we can't turn her over that way."

The minute he said it, I knew that was the right answer, and I was chagrined that I hadn't thought of it myself.

So we tied the blouses together as Tony had suggested, worked around to the other side and pulled, and boom! —over she came, with a homely thwack on the water.

"You stay here and hold her down, while I get aboard on the other side," I said.

In the raft, I pulled the boys aboard by the wrists one at a time, and for the moment our troubles were over. I looked around and reflected that it was swell to be alive, though why I should have thought that then I don't know.

[4]

As we huddled together in the darkness trying to keep warm while the wind held our clammy clothes against us, we were not downhearted. I had confidence in the raft's ability to stay afloat, and the boys were sure we would be rescued in the morning. There was much complaining over the loss of our cigarettes and matches, which had of course been ruined in our long immersion. I too would have liked a cigarette, but most of all I wanted a cup of hot coffee.

We settled down to rest as best we could until dawn, but we soon learned that we could not sleep. The raft was only four feet long by eight feet wide. With its sides inflated like tires, it resembled an oblong doughnut. The dimensions inside were eighty inches by forty inches. We discovered almost at once that it was impossible for three men to dispose this space so that any one of us would be comfortable.

Tony lay most of the night in the bottom of the boat, his spirits seeming to rise and fall like the sea beneath us. Sometimes he would talk cheerfully, almost gaily, and then he would lapse into a depressing silence, in which his gloomy thoughts could be felt by Gene and me, as we felt the darkness of the night.

Gene perched on the gunwale, occasionally moving restlessly. He had been brought up in a rural community, and chafed at confinement. He stood up to stretch occasionally, but found it hard to keep his balance with his feet pushing that thin rubber floor against the sea beneath as into a cushion.

We passed a long night, it seemed. Our conversation, when we talked, consisted mostly of reassurance, repeated and repeated, that a plane or ship would find us in the morning. I hoped so, and pretended confidence.

Day approached imperceptibly until suddenly it was dawn, in the abrupt way of the tropics. All at once the sea appeared, a leaden gray; then little white tongues of fire danced on the waves, and the east became a conflagration that resolved itself into a pleasant, rising ball, the sun. Before this, as soon as the sky had taken misty form, we three were straining our eyes for sight of a rescue ship or plane.

The boys discussed every possibility with cheerful eagerness. They were confident that many ships were scouring every square mile of this area to find us. If we weren't found today, they agreed, help would surely come tomorrow.

But I was not so sure. I was an old head in this business, and I knew that our admiral could not risk his entire force in a doubtful attempt to rescue three men. After all, we were at war. We were in the vicinity of known enemy positions and naval forces. There would be one quick look, and then we must be given up for lost.

This would be a bitter pill for the boys to swallow. But it was only simple, military logic.

My thoughts were not gloomy, but they were hard, and I kept them to myself.

A moment came when I thought the boys were right and I was wrong, to my great relief.

I judged it to be about 8:00 or 8:30 A.M. when we sighted the plane. At first I thought it was a bird, but far away as it was we could see that it was steady on its course, and in a few minutes we heard the faint sound of motors.

We jumped to our feet in our excitement, and almost tipped over the raft.

"Hey, take it easy, there," I ordered sternly. "We've still got plenty of time to drown!"

I didn't have to issue a second warning. We sat down carefully, keeping our eyes on the plane. She was from our own forces, all right.

We looked at our watches, but they had all stopped at 7:40, evidently the moment our plane dropped from under us and we went into the water. I opened the face of my watch and lifted out the works. They were already corroded beyond repair.

It was plain that we were being hunted. The plane approached on an easterly course at about 140 knots, never deviating from her line of flight. As she came nearer, we began to wave our arms, but there was no sign that we were seen.

Then Gene and Tony began to shout. I wished we had been able to save one of the parachutes. I would have opened it now and let it billow on the water. I made one quick search of the raft. There was not a single thing that we could use as a signaling device, except our shirts. Gene and Tony already had theirs off and were waving them wildly. Their voices were becoming hoarse from shouting.

Evidently our tiny raft, being orange-yellow in color, was invisible in the silver path of the morning sun on the sea. The plane came closer, and closer, until she was within a half a mile of us.

Finally it was clear that we had not been seen. The plane was going away now, the sound of her motors dwindling to the southward like the last note of a dirge.

I sank down upon the forward thwart. Gene and Tony were leaning by their hands on the sides, still waving halfheartedly, and staring as if their thoughts could bring him back.

Now the plane was a speck in the sky, and the only sound was the lapping of the waves against the raft. Then the speck was gone, and we felt terribly alone in the immensity of sky and sea, and sun.

The boys sank down, their faces expressionless.

I have been sorry that I said what I did then; it was automatic, I guess, and I didn't even remember until Tony recalled it later, bitterly:

"Boys, there goes our one and only chance."

CHAPTER · TWO

SOMETIMES, on our long brooding watches when we skidded southward in a following sea, I remembered my last meal on the carrier. There was the usual chaff in the chief petty officers' mess but I, Harold F. Dixon, aviation chief machinist's mate in the United States Navy, ate mostly in silence. Our 11-o'clock chow that was, and in three hours I was taking up a small bomber in the routine scouting. I rose and turned to go to the ready room, where the pilots get their wind data and plot their navigation. Then I stopped at the door, turned, and looked back at the table.

We had had celery that day. Most men preferred the tender celery hearts but I have always liked the hard outer stalks. Without thinking of anything in particular, I walked back to the table, took two more stalks of celery, and ate them slowly. As I reflected on this later, it seemed to me that I was under some compul-

sion to stoke my body for an ordeal to come. I have
thought many times that this was a strange and fortunate thing I did, for that luncheon was to be my last
meal for thirty-four days. I had occasion to wish that
my premonition, if premonition it was, had gone a
little further and made me take an extra swallow of
water.

Going past the sick bay I was stopped by a first-class
pharmacist's mate.

"Want to see something?" he asked me.

"Yes," I said.

He said, "I have a friend of yours in here," and
opened the door.

I looked in, and there was this fellow lying flat on
his back in bed. His arms and legs were waving back
and forth in the air, and he was talking to himself.

This man was a very good friend of mine. He had a
very dangerous job on the ship, and he and I discussed
several times his chances of getting hurt. In fact, we
had been talking about this a day or two previous. He
told me what he was going to do in case a certain wire
broke. And by golly, this particular morning something
did happen—I don't know why—and he got his head
cracked very hard on the landing.

He was just standing at his place, and whether this
wire broke or not I never found out, but anyway his
skull was crushed very badly.

I had that funny lift in my stomach. I had a feeling that something was going to happen.

The doctors were there, trying to give him an examination. He was babbling. You couldn't make out his words; his voice just went on and on, rising sharply and then falling to a whisper.

I said to the first-class pharmacist's mate:

"Think he will live?"

The pharmacist's mate didn't say what he thought. He just shook his head.

That funny feeling came again. I thought to myself: I'm going to be in exactly that same position. I could see myself lying flat on my back with my legs in the air.

Then the thought came to me: This fellow is suffering, by the way he is groaning; mentally there is something very badly wrong with him and his subconscious mind knows that.

I thought: I'm going to do all my suffering before my mind goes out, and that will be the climax.

My wife and I believe in spiritualism—we're very ardent spiritualists. I've had these premonitions, and I had another right then and there. I used to go up and take my exercise walking the deck of the blacked-out carrier, and sometimes lately I'd look at the white foam thrown by our wake on a long black swell, and feel somehow uneasy. I took these long walks every night, and calisthenics every morning, deliberately keeping my body fit. I think Gene Aldrich and Tony Pastula did the same. We were in the best of health, all three of us, and I think that's why we came through our ordeal.

January 16th was the day—January 16, 1942. I walked up to the ready room and went about my business to stand by. The hop wasn't to take off for a couple of hours—I think I still had two and a half hours to wait. I always spend my time in the ready room; it's a regular hangout for pilots, because there is where we get all our military data. Everything from the bridge comes down there—all the wind dope, likely enemy dispositions, the last word on everything the bridge knows that might help a pilot.

I can't tell much about the ship, or what we were doing. We were on a war mission. There's a discretion to be observed. Anyway, I went to the ready room. I was not required to be there until an hour before take-off, but I went up right after lunch. I don't remember talking to anyone.

The wind data was starting to come in, and the pilots paid close attention. This day the winds were variable, and didn't seem to hold in any one direction. First the aerologist would send down the data on wind from one direction of a given course. In about ten minutes there would be another direction of wind. There were probably half a dozen changes of wind in that last hour I was there. That's quite variable.

All the talk was on navigation. It is customary in the squadron that the pilots check each other's navigation problems. One of the officers wasn't going out, and he checked on mine. We get the wind and other data (I'd rather not go into detail about this, and much of it is mathematical) and work out a problem in navigation, and that's what we go by in the air.

We each worked out my problem—this officer and I—but in the meantime they stuck up about three changes of wind in the last half hour. We finally agreed on a likely direction of the wind, and I had just finished my problem when word was passed to man the planes. There's no wasting time here. The pilots dash right up to the flight deck and prepare to take off.

My bomber was standing ready. We were looking for Jap submarines. I guess it's all right to say that. Submarines are where you find them.

The young sailor standing by my plane was to be the bomber with me. The gunner was in the plane. We had three cockpits. I was forward, Tony Pastula, the bomber, in the middle cockpit, and the gunner behind. That was Gene Aldrich, as it turned out. I didn't see Gene until the next morning, as a matter of fact. When we went in the water I was busy, and then it was dark, but later on we introduced ourselves with more or less formality. I get a bomber and a gunner, and this time it happened to be Pastula and Aldrich. Later Tony said he had made a couple of hops with me before, but I don't remember. Aldrich I had seen around. He knew me a little better than Tony did. Gene flew all the time.

When I was not flying or in the ready room, my job on the ship was in the educational department. I had been running this for many years, and it required most of my time. I instructed Aldrich, along with other boys, in radio and different subjects. I remembered instructing him, but always in a group with several others, so I had never paid much attention to him as an individual. The three of us just knew each other's last names and rates.

There's always some excitement for me in taking off from a carrier. If you don't feel it you can't be a born flier, that's all. There are shouted orders, and the whole ship seems to come alive when all those motors begin to growl. All the things a pilot has to check, there's no sitting back to enjoy the show—and a show it is!—but I feel a tug inside and something swells like the roar of the crowd at a football game when they kick off. Maybe it's more like the start of an auto race, when the flag comes down and the noises rise and then everything begins to move—and the broad, bright flight deck falls away—you're up!

We took off at about 2:15 P.M. and proceeded on our mission. I could see a plane to the left and another to the right as I went out. As I said, we were on a scouting hop, looking for enemy submarines or surface vessels. The day was clear, with scattered clouds. "Scattered clouds"—that's technical language with us. It means that approximately one-fourth of the sky is obscured, with clouds here and there. These were bright white cumulus clouds against a sharp blue sky. The sunlight had that glassiness peculiar to the tropics, and put a glare on the almost purple sea. Everything looked fine.

This flight was to take us to the maximum range of our aircraft—not to be too definite about it. At the end of our outward leg I looked off to the right, and then checked the altitude. The sun was probably 45 minutes high yet. There were two very large rain squalls, one to the right and one to the left, and I passed right between. I could see the sun under the cloud formation. It made a very heavy, golden glow on the water. I figured that the ship should be out in that direction, to the left, but the sunlight made the water like looking into a yellow flame.

It was getting to be time to look.

I called on the interphone.

"Pastula, can you take a drift sight?"

You do that with an instrument, which I needn't go into here, as it is military.

Tony answered, "Yes, sir."

Tony was a mechanic. He was supposed to take these things apart and put them together again. So when he answered, there was no question in my mind that he could take a drift sight.

I called for a wind estimate, and then called again for a check. Wind estimates are tricky things—even the best bombardier can go wrong on one, and conditions were none too good for such an estimate. But, when the same answer came back the second time I figured it was probably correct. If so, the ship should be to the right. If the estimate was wrong, the ship should be to the left. I decided I should take the wind estimate as being correct, and turned to the right for a search. I wasn't particularly worried. I still had some safety factor. But I knew something had gone wrong, and that I had missed the ship.

The two boys also knew by this time, and from our maneuvers, that we had missed the ship. However, we hadn't started to worry. There had been no conversation between us; our only communication was by means of the interphone, and talking is strictly confined to the business of the flight.

Until now it had been a dull afternoon. We hadn't seen anything that looked like an enemy, so the boys had had a little workout with our practice ammunition and dummy bombs which we carry for this purpose. Now I dropped real bombs, to get rid of their weight, and then made for altitude. The next business was to get a bearing back to the ship by radio.

I called the ship for a bearing. There was no answer. I called, and called again. Silence.

By this time I knew we were becoming hopelessly lost. The gas was just about running out.

Grasping at a straw, I turned the plane and steamed on until the gas was down to ten gallons. This would keep us in the air only a few minutes.

I passed back word to stand by for a landing in the water. I had no recourse left.

These carrier-based bombers are land planes, of course. They are not built to float, but one can at least expect the plane to stay on top of the water the time it takes to inflate the rubber life raft, stow the emergency gear in it, get aboard and shove clear. The raft is folded and tucked into a small cover, and is standard equipment for planes of this sort. It is inflated by opening a valve to a tiny flask of carbon dioxide. The thing works in very much the same way as a home-charging seltzer water outfit. When the valve is cracked the imprisoned gas rushes into the inflation compartment of the raft and expands, blowing up the raft like an inner tube with a thin blanket of the same rubberized fabric covering the hole, to make a floor.

"Pastula," I called back on the phone, "bring the rations, water, life raft, and anything useful you can get hold of. Here, take these—" I passed him my chart board, automatic pistol and shells that were in my pocket, and a pair of pliers.

"Bring the parachute," I added.

Aldrich was to furnish the first-aid kit, signaling devices, and any other loose gear that might be valuable to us.

"I'm going to make a landing in the water," I told him, "and wait for them to come back and find us. Ready, Aldrich? Pastula?"

"Ready," said Aldrich.

"All set," from Tony.

Their voices were calm.

I squared away then, into the wind, to make a power-stall landing. The sea was calm and slaty. The sun had just set, and darkness was rising in the sky to the eastward.

CHAPTER · THREE

WE had expected the plane to float for at least a few minutes, but she sank almost immediately.

The wing on which I had been squatting dropped from under me without a warning ripple, and the weighted nose as quickly pulled the fuselage beneath the slate-gray sea, leaving a tiny whirlpool to mark its grave.

Pastula and Aldrich floated straight up out of their cockpits, pulled by their pneumatic life jackets as if hoisted by slings beneath their arms. And I was wrestling desperately with the rubber raft, now inflating in my hands.

Aldrich was hanging onto my chart board, which Tony had passed to him, and two flashlights. He lit one just as the plane sank with that incredible finality of a dropping stone. Seconds later, I heard him strangling in the salt water, and saw the lighted flashlight spiraling

down under the water like a luminous fish. In an instant
it was gone, and we were in darkness.

In his first racking struggle to keep afloat in this terrifying new element—I learned later that neither he nor
Tony could swim—Aldrich dropped the chart board,
as well as both flashlights. The parachutes had proved
impossible to salvage. I unshipped my .45 automatic to
get rid of the weight which was pulling me down, and
Aldrich did the same. Tony Pastula saved his, though
against his will, because it was fastened around his thigh
by a rawhide loop which he was unable to loose in the
water. Meanwhile we were all swallowing great quantities of sea.

At first, after we were all three safe aboard the raft,
we wondered whether it was going to be strong enough
to withstand the terrific pounding it was taking from
the waves. Then I recalled that a friend of mine had once
floated for nine days in the same type of craft, off
Panama. After that, I was not so concerned about the
raft's sinking.

I talked to the boys about our chances of rescue, and
tried to cheer them up. This didn't take as long as I
had expected. I learned that healthy young men in
their early twenties are not naturally pessimistic. Gene
and Tony's husky young bodies, hardened in the navy,
threw off the exhaustion of their struggle in the sea.
The discipline in which they had been trained exerted

itself now, and they were ready to appraise the situation calmly.

We thought about the things you would expect a person to think about under such circumstances. We were on a spot, and knew it. However, we confidently expected the ship to send back a search, and we knew there was a good possibility that we'd be found.

Tony was actually elated now.

"Chief"—he called me Chief throughout the voyage —"when I found out you were gonna land in that water, I thought, Boy, this is it!"

"You thought I couldn't land that plane in the water, eh?"

If that sounds like a smug statement, well, I probably was a little pleased with myself. That was a good landing, although it wasn't difficult to make.

Tony was giggling in his relief to be alive.

"Boy, chief, I thought we was goners for sure! I thought we was gonna fly in a thousand pieces! Best I hoped for was that I wouldn't know what hit me. Chief, how'd ya do it?"

I explained that it wasn't difficult, nor dangerous.

Tony whistled and laughed. He felt pretty good about the whole situation.

I turned to Aldrich and asked him a few questions about the radio set. I couldn't understand why we had been unable to raise the ship. I thought we should have caught a signal.

"Hey, who's got a cigarette?" Tony demanded.

Gene jammed his hand into his sodden trousers pocket with automatic politeness, and then stopped and grinned.

"I'd like a cigarette with my coffee, if we had some coffee," he drawled.

The lack of cigarettes and coffee was to become one of our favorite topics of conversation. We navy men like our coffee good and strong, with plenty of sugar, and most of all we like it often. I think we missed our smokes and coffee more than anything else.

Meanwhile I looked over the raft as best I could, and felt all over the fabric, wishing Gene had hung onto one of those flashlights. However, I examined the boat thoroughly, and found it to be in practically new condition and in excellent shape, which pleased me very much. I found out later that the boat was about five years old; you can see it now in the naval museum at Annapolis. Incidentally, I've got to write to the Goodyear people.

We didn't do a lot of talking that night, but discussed our predicament. Tony's high spirits had dimmed somewhat, and he was lying in the bottom of the boat, his head on Gene's feet and mine wedged into his back.

I had taken an inventory of our equipment, and tried to belittle its insufficiency by pointing out that we were sure to be rescued in the morning.

We found to our sorrow that all the necessary tools

—oars, pump, and so forth—were missing. The pump was to blow up the boat if we developed a leak. When I discovered that we had no pump, my thoughts might have been a prayer if I hadn't been too shocked to form words in my mind.

We found that all we had was this:

A police whistle; and

A small mirror and a pair of pliers, which were in the tool pocket of the boat;

Another pair of pliers that I had stuck in my pocket and which broke the first time I attempted to use them;

An ordinary pocketknife—Gene's;

A can of rubber cement patching fluid, for which I found use;

A small piece of patching material;

A .45 caliber pistol which Pastula had saved;

Three clips of ammunition;

Two pneumatic life jackets;

And the clothing we had on.

The two lads threw their shoes away, as I was afraid shoes would scuff the boat, and also because we needed the space. They threw them away the next day, but we regretted that later. I kept my shoes, thinking we had better save one pair; in case we made a desert island we wouldn't want to be entirely without shoes.

Tony fortunately had a dungaree jacket over his shirt, which gave us an extra garment. This came in very handy later, as we used his shirt for rags and he wore the dungaree jacket.

We were, or at least pretended to be, very optimistic this first night as we talked over the situation.

"We'll keep a watch," I said. "Watch on, watch off, and relax in between."

It was a four-hour watch the first night, one of us keeping a sharp lookout constantly in case something came back. None of us could more than doze; although the sea was calm, there were always tiny surface waves, looking innocent as a ripple in your bathtub, but each a sharp explosion when it hit beneath the boat with maddening regularity. We bobbled like a cork, and to me one of the most amazing phases of this adventure was that we never became seasick.

Each little wave that struck the bottom of our rubber bubble of a boat was a jarring blow across the shoulders and the back of the head of the man lying inside. Imagine doubling up on a tiny mattress, with the strongest man you know striking the underside as hard as he could with a baseball bat, twice every three seconds, while someone else hurls buckets of cold salt water in your face. That's what it was like.

So it was a waking night we spent, and when we talked it was to go over and over the same situation with the monotonous insistence of three men with a single all-engrossing predicament. None of us lay down very long, though, as I said, Tony later seemed to become used to it.

"Hey, look, it's dawn!"

I don't remember who said it, but we gave a cheer, and immediately began joking about breakfast. It was then we found out how much Gene liked cheese, and he was never to let us forget it. Whenever we talked about food, and food was almost our only topic of conversation in the days and nights to come, Gene put cheese on everything. Once he and Tony talked for two hours about ham and cheese sandwiches in every possible variety, while I fought down my growing temper and tried to join in affably with my own suggestions and remembrances. Every time Gene mentioned eating, he would add cheese to it. He'd say, "I'd like to have a dozen fried eggs with a nice big slice of cheese melted over the top for breakfast." He could think of more things with cheese.

The sun came in like an old friend, and we felt suddenly like three schoolboys up early in the morning for some youthful promised thrill. We chattered and shifted unwisely about the raft, and scanned our vast, expanding world for sign of ship or plane. Three can do a lot of looking, and we needed all our eyes.

CHAPTER · FOUR

THEN the plane came; and went.

We sank back, spent by our futile effort to attract the pilot. Tony and I were facing each other from opposite sides of the raft. Gene sat on the after thwart. He was still gazing hopefully after the speeding scout—now rapidly becoming smaller. Tony was watching me.

For a moment my heart was in the lowest possible depths. I can quote exactly what I said—"Boys, there goes our one and only chance"—for Tony weeks later recalled to me every word. With that single statement I almost killed the hope in Tony's game soul, for the time being. He did not realize then that I still had cards to play.

Gene was by no means dispirited. "Shucks, maybe he saw us and is going back for help," he suggested confidently. He was enthusiastic all day. He expected any minute to see a destroyer, or another plane.

I had made one slip, and was careful not to make another. So I agreed heartily with Gene, and never mentioned what was in my mind. All that day I lied cheerfully, and let the boys think we had a good chance to be rescued. Secretly I was taking stock of our position with a view to sailing that tiny raft, without oars or sails, to the nearest friendly island. Our situation was complicated by the possibility that certain islands in the vicinity might now be in the possession of the Japanese. I had no illusions as to what would happen to us all if we fell into the hands of enemies on some remote atoll.

Despite his low spirits at the moment, the tenacity for life in Tony's stanch Polish nature asserted itself quickly and he began to consider practical means of making our situation better. He paid no more attention to the sky, but silently searched in the inside of the raft with his eyes. He began rummaging in the oar pocket.

"Ah!" he exclaimed with satisfaction.

He held a mirror of stainless steel, placed in the oar pocket obviously as a heliographic signaling device. For the rest of the day Tony practiced with the mirror, flashing it in the sun, so he would know how to use it if the occasion arose.

Tony liked anything that required him to use his hands. He had taken a mechanics course in high school, and after the war, when he leaves the navy, he hopes to work in a machine factory.

The newspaper accounts of our voyage only mentioned Tony briefly, as "Anthony J. Pastula, 24, aviation
ordnanceman second class, of 149 Ellenwood Avenue,
Youngstown, Ohio." The news was in the adventure,
not the men—but men make adventure just as much as
adventure makes men. Through coming to know Tony,
in the long days and nights ahead, I obtained a better
understanding of these sons of "foreigners" who form
such a large percentage of the young men who sail our
ships and planes and man our guns.

Tony's parents came from Poland; neither his father
nor his mother speaks English at home. His father is a
landscape gardener, now caretaker of an estate in
Youngstown which belongs to a prominent newspaper
publisher there. Tony helped his father, spare time and
summers, until he "got tired of depending on the folks,"
and joined the navy. Before that he had been in the
Civilian Conservation Corps. Gene Aldrich was a CCC
boy too. Neither he nor Tony had any background of
the sea. I, of course, had long training on the sea which
was to stand me in good stead here, but my business
now is flying.

Tony, like many others, joined the navy in 1939 because he believed his country would soon be at war.
Previous to that his contacts with the military had been
with the army. Among his jobs in the CCC during his
two hitches of 1937 and 1938 was driving army convoy
trucks.

Tony had a stern independence in his nature which brought him steeply around two milestones in his young life. One was when he left school.

"This course, I was doing all right, see?" Tony explained. "I didn't expect no A, but I thought I oughta get a B or anyways a C, and that woulda been all right. I never cared about making the best marks in school, see, long as I learned the stuff. Well, I had that course down good, and when I got that report card and saw that big shiny F, I just said—"

Never mind what he said; he just walked out of that senior high school and never went back.

The other crisis concerned religion. Tony had been brought up in the Catholic faith. The only prayers he knew were in Polish. We all did some praying on this trip, first because it worked a couple of times and we were willing to keep trying again, and later because it gave us something regular to do. In fact, our "prayer meeting" was to become the high spot of our evenings.

Tony was good-humored about religion. "I quit, see? This night I was standing around the corner with the fellas and this preacher comes along, and I don't pay much attention, and then this preacher goes and talks about me because I don't tip my cap to him. Made me sore." So Tony, disgusted, would have nothing more to do with formal religion.

Aldrich, on the other hand, had a deep streak of piety.

His brother was a preacher. It was Gene who suggested our prayer meetings.

Gene is more of a farm boy; his home is in Sikeston, Missouri. He is younger than Tony, just twenty-two, and had been in the navy only fifteen months. He had put in some time in the CCC as a cook, and for our "meals," as we became really hungry, he cooked us many hypothetical dinners, with Tony, who for a time had been a "sandwich man" in the C's, offering suggestions. Before the trip was over Gene was talking seriously about trying for a transfer to the navy cooks' department, and I think he will.

Cooking played a large part in Gene's early life. His father was a railroader, a section foreman, and Gene recalled that it used to be a favorite stunt of his and his father's to go out about four o'clock in the morning to shoot squirrels for their breakfast. It seems there are a lot of squirrels in Missouri.

One of Gene's concerns on the trip was a $5,000 life insurance policy he had taken in favor of his mother. He wondered if she had been able to get it yet. Money was scarce around Gene's home. Gene joined the navy after finding that he didn't like the CCC. The spirit of adventure got him, and he thought he could do better and get more schooling in the navy. He had had one year of high school, working to put himself through.

Talking it over, Gene shook his head quizzically. "If Mother could see me now!"

Well, she wouldn't have liked the look of it. The wind this morning was in the southeast, blowing us toward a group of islands which we presumed to be deserted. However, we thought the Japanese might have put some men there, so we were not enthusiastic about making these islands, on that account.

I was concerned at once about learning to control the raft, figuring out ways and means of working toward the larger islands that I knew to be in friendly hands.

The geography of this part of the Pacific was far from a mystery to me. Every day in the ready room I had studied the charts, and had a mental picture of where every island was. So I knew from the beginning just where I wanted to go. I had no intention of letting that raft drift aimlessly, guided only by the shifting winds. We were without rudder, oars or canvas, but still I was determined to sail that raft if I could. And I maintain that I did sail it. I worked like the devil to sail it, and I resent anyone's saying we "drifted."

Controlling our craft's progress was my first concern because, while we were entirely without food or water, there was nothing any of us could do about this but wait for the Lord to send us a shower, and bring some food where we could catch it. I figured the Lord would help those who helped themselves, so I set out immediately to take every bit of advantage that I could of the few materials available to me.

The wind blew up to a fresh breeze of about 12 knots, and I spent most of the first day observing how our boat was going to act. I knew from the previous experiences both of myself and of several shipmates who had tried these boats in the water that, being flat and smooth-bottomed, the raft would sail along smartly in the wind. It soon became apparent that the raft was not only responding satisfactorily to the push of the wind, but that she had no tendency to yaw. She remained steadily lengthwise of the trough of the sea.

Thus the raft presented her entire length to the force of the wind, with the inflated sides acting as a sail of sorts.

About eighteen hours after we went into the water, the wind shifted to the northwest and started driving us south. We were still in the hands of the fates and had to go with the winds. There were islands directly on our course now, but we were afraid the Japs had taken possession of these. We were not at all anxious to fall into their hands, as we believed they were in no mood to take prisoners of war, even castaways.

CHAPTER · FIVE

A SERIOUS lack was head covering; the sun's rays came down like red-hot corkscrews and cooked our brains. The days were horribly hot. Tony had his dungaree jacket, so I took his shirt and tore out the two front panels. With these I fashioned a sort of bonnet which gave the top of our heads some protection from the tropical sun. Occasionally we dunked these rags in the sea, so that the wind, striking them, would keep our heads cool.

There was no way to protect our faces. From mid-morning to late afternoon the whole sky was a blue glare of heat which the sun threw back, intensified. At times, when the sea was calm, the rubber raft became unbearably hot to the touch. Our only relief was to keep flicking sea water on it and ourselves.

We wet our clothes almost constantly. Within fifteen minutes after a good dousing they would be thoroughly dry again. After we had soaked our clothes three or four times they would be stiff as boards from the salt, which added no little to our discomfort. Then we would have to take our garments off and rinse them in the sea to get out some of the salt. It was a tiresome, never-ending chore.

Nights, especially when the sea was rough, we had opposite problems. Then our wet garments were clammy and cold. The two of us who were not on watch would huddle together to conserve our bodily heat. We spared our energy as much as possible. These discomforts, which we had to bear without food, water or sleep, soon began to fray our dispositions, but we all realized our predicament, and we knew that losing our tempers would be of no possible benefit. We kept forcibly choking back our growing irritability with each other. This was at times an almost heroic feat.

On the first day I shot off a whole clip of ammunition—about half our supply—trying to kill a bird. We thought it was going to be easy to shoot a bird, because the curious creatures flocked around us by the hundreds, coming so close to inspect our strange craft that we were almost under the illusion that we could reach up and grab one. Actually, they came down within five or six feet of us.

I held the pistol until a bird was directly overhead, then I would aim and let go. These birds were fearless, and we soon had to admit that they were in little danger from us. The boat bobbled like a cork, and this seemed to throw off my aim every time. The best I could do was knock feathers from a few, so I finally gave up.

We were very much interested in the birds and the various tropical fishes. The boat, being orange-yellow in color, was a great attraction to the fish, and they all came up and looked it over as if it were some strange animal.

Evidently the birds had the same idea. All day they coasted slowly over our heads, always approaching upwind, and peering curiously down at this odd-appearing floating object that had invaded their exclusive world of wind and water.

There was one kind, a snow-white little fellow, which seemed to ignore us completely. There were always two or three of these in company. First one would let out a sort of croaking chirp, then another would answer. They had short, rounded, bullet-shaped bodies which appeared to be about the size of that of a bobwhite quail. They had three tail feathers about two feet long, which hung out behind them like streamers, giving a very graceful effect to their flight.

They would climb up to two or three hundred feet altitude and look around for their prey on the water. When they sighted it they would make a vertical dive, shooting straight down and making a headlong plunge into the water, looking for all the world like a dive bomber launching a bomb at the enemy. I sometimes wondered why the little fellows didn't pop wide open when they hit the water, but it didn't seem to faze them.

Watching these birds, the albatrosses and terns of all kinds, banqueting liberally all day long from this unfriendly sea that was so barren for us, whetted our appetites and made us angry with ourselves that we were helpless to obtain food where less reasoning creatures plundered and gorged.

Aldrich showed at once that he was interested in fishing, so we looked around for something to use for a line. In the tool pocket there was a three-strand cotton cord perhaps fifteen feet long. This I unraveled into three thinner pieces of line, and cut them off to about ten feet. Tony had a red bandanna handkerchief, so Gene tied a piece of this to the end of the string for bait, as we had heard that tropical fish would bite at anything of bright color.

Gene stood over the side and flung his line into the water. It was over for only a couple of minutes when he discovered that the bait was gone—bitten clean off. We then rigged a piece of wire as a leader, put on another piece of rag, and attached a piece of the broken pliers to weight it down.

I broke the pliers trying to make a fishhook from a spring in the ammunition clip. As I took hold of the wire and clamped down, the bolt that holds the two sections of pliers together gave way, having crystallized. However, the piece of broken plier made a good sinker. With this rig Gene fished for hours, but never had another bite. He tried all kinds of schemes, discoursing the while on his experiences fishing back home, near the Mississippi River.

Tony, not to be outdone as a conversationalist, chimed in, whenever the subject was remotely appropriate, with reminiscences of the work he had done at home helping his father as a landscape gardener. This particular theme was always welcomed by me on its frequent recurrences, for I could ring in something about my avocado ranch ("Calavo," 1¼ acres), at La Mesa, near San Diego. That was about the nearest we came to having common conversational interests, except when we talked about coffee.

The three of us were almost constant coffee drinkers, like practically all men-o'-warsmen. While we missed our cigarettes at first, we were now missing our coffee badly and as time went on we were to long for it constantly. We eventually got over our craving for cigarettes to some extent, but I missed my daily ration of six to eight cups of coffee—and I mean *coffee*. There is no better zip-giver in the world than a good cup of coffee with sugar and cream when you are low.

We made a game of our hardships as time went on. Talking about food and cigarettes and coffee of course accentuated our longings, but paradoxically we seemed to derive some comfort from thus torturing ourselves. We talked about food, particularly, for hours, often wistfully, but sometimes making a jest of it.

Tony, who had a sense of humor, soon devised a favorite way to start or end all conversation. He would turn suddenly to Gene (whom he called Henry, after his favorite radio character), and order with a mischievous grin:

"Come on, Henry—time to put on the pot!"

"Henry" and I never failed to enter into the spirit of the game, with elaborate suggestions for the making and pouring of the coffee. We frequently adopted ludicrously exaggerated drawing-room tones and gestures for this ritual, broadly burlesquing what we fondly believed was the true Park Avenue manner.

Later, I think, it must have been this continual practice of deliberate idiocy that kept us from going really insane in our exposure, starvation, and thirst.

CHAPTER · SIX

SO far I had no means of controlling our progress. I thought, anyway, that it was vital to keep track of our position. To do this it was necessary to devise a way to gauge, as accurately as possible, the speed of our craft. The only navigation instrument I had was a small aerial navigator's scale of mileage. This was handy, and of course I had a thorough knowledge of the heavenly bodies used in navigation.

I tried several schemes for estimating our speed. One of the first was to throw a piece of rag, which was the only thing we had that would float, into the water, then counting by the one-thousand-and-one, one-thousand-and-two method, it taking just about a second to say each numeral. While we still had plenty of rags I would tear a few threads and cast them into the water, as far ahead as I could, then count as they passed the length of the raft, which was the known factor.

Thus I came to deduce that an estimated 12 knots

of wind gave us a drift of approximately 2.5 knots, six knots of wind a drift of one knot.

However, I did not find the thread method very satisfactory. In the tool pocket there was also a 20-foot length of heavy cord. I cut off a length of about six feet of this, and tied to the end a flat metal identification disk from Tony's key ring, to act as a sinker. I tied the other end of the line to the center of the side of the raft, and tossed it out to drift. The metal disk was slightly concave and would flutter as we scooted along. The faster we went, the faster it would flutter, and the nearer the surface it would rise. I soon became quite expert at computing our speed with fair accuracy by this means.

I figured that if I could estimate our speed and direction within a ten per cent error, we would at least not become entirely lost in the time it would take us to starve to death or be overtaken by disaster from one of the other ever-present hazards we were facing daily.

At the very first we decided to keep a continuous watch, and we did throughout the first few weeks—up until the time we became too weak and exhausted to sit up for any length of time.

We had no timepiece, of course, but each of us would stand what we judged to be four hours, at the start. After about a week I cut this to two hours. Naturally our minds began to dull, and our faculties for judgment became less and less dependable, so there developed considerable reneging on the watchtime. Once I stood watch practically all day by myself in the blazing sun, and after that I laid down the law in no uncertain terms. The watches worked out more satisfactorily after that.

Discipline was well kept throughout the voyage. Naturally I was in command. I took an occasion to remind the boys that I as captain held absolute authority.

"We've got to be all for one and one for all," I explained, "but when a final decision has to be made by one of us for us all, the captain's word has got to be the law."

Tony and Gene, good sailors both, readily assented, and we had no trouble on that score.

As time went on, though, our dispositions became rottener and rottener. I, being older and more experienced, blame myself more than either of the others for the times toward the last when my temper got out of control. There were occasions, I'm ashamed to admit, when my greatest exasperation was over the fact that I had nothing in the boat to throw. On the whole, though, we managed to get along very well, and even had some pleasant times with such little diversions as we could invent.

The boys were both pretty much afraid at first that our boat would soon spring a leak and sink. Without the air pump, which was lost with the plane, we had no means whatever of keeping up the air pressure if any leak developed. I'll admit that I was none too happy about this situation at times.

I kept warning the boys to be careful about fraying or inadvertently snagging the fabric with any sharp metal, or the buttons on their clothes. It was all-important that we show the greatest possible care for the sides of the air compartments of our boat. So we were as cautious as could be, knowing it would be much easier to maintain the boat in its present excellent condition than to try to recondition it should we puncture the sides through careless maneuvering. To this end I found it necessary to repeat frequently my warnings of the danger attendant from shirt and trousers buttons, careless handling of gear, and even quick and incautious moving of our persons, which would cause unnecessary scuffing or wearing of the fabric.

Occasionally I would dig in the tool pocket for the small bottle of rubber cement, and touch up any frayed spots where it looked as if the fabric might be weakening in the vicinity. This treatment not only retarded the fraying action on those parts, but showed us the spots that were most vulnerable to wear owing to our moving about in the boat.

As time went on and our gallant little rubberized fabric boat showed no signs of serious wear, or deterioration of any kind, I soon acquired the greatest of confidence in her. She rode the waves like a veteran ocean-going steamer.

The only time she would take water to any important amount was when a big comber broke directly into the boat. Then about five to ten gallons of white water would pour down on us from the break of the crest. That always meant a good soaking of everything in the boat, including us, and a job of bailing out again.

The bailing we accomplished by taking off our clothes, sopping up the water with them and wringing them out over the side, then wringing out our clothes again before putting them back on.

When the wind had held steadily in one direction for a period of a few hours, all the swells and surface waves would run in the same direction, quite evenly and with a steady motion. Every sixth or seventh wave would be the big one that broke. After that everything would die down to a lull—then start building up to another breaker. These gave us very little trouble until the wind got up to around 20 knots, and the breakers became heavy.

But just after a shift of wind it would be a different story. The big swells would run with the former wind direction, but the surface waves, being wind-formed, would now be going in a new direction. When these opposing forces met, there was terrifying commotion which resulted in many nasty drenchings.

When off watch and lying in the bottom of the boat trying to get some rest, it would be more than annoying to get a face full of cold and heavy salt water, thrown with the force of a bludgeon. Because of this and also because of the smaller waves which were continually punching at the thin cover of fabric that formed our bottom, it was impossible to get anything approaching rest except during the latter hours of a protracted, dead calm, when all surface waves had died down. These periods were rare, and gave us other things to worry about.

The second day we had time to appreciate the dawn. When the big tropical sun ball peeked over the gray horizon, our dismal world became instantly beautiful, and our drooping spirits never failed to lift.

Tony would sing out, "Time to put on the pot!"— and Gene and I never lost a second in searching with our eyes the farthest blue and gold reaches of our suddenly expanded ken. It was at dawning that we stretched our stiffened muscles, and worked warm new life into numb and aching members. It was always then that our spirits were at their highest, for each new day brought new hope, and new variation to relieve the long monotony of the cheerless night.

This good humor usually lasted until the friendly sun shortly turned into a malevolent brass ball of heat that baked us pitilessly inside our wet clothes like fish wrapped in leaves to broil.

At about noon this second day we could stand it no longer without taking the last measure for relief that was left. We stripped then, and, one at a time, slipped into the water, holding the side of the boat. Each of us stayed in about five minutes, dunking up and down.

It made us feel so much better that we then decided to keep deliberately wet during the heat of the day, flicking water on each other. We had our swim in quite gingerly fashion, losing no time hopping back into the boat, for there were a lot of sharks around. We talked this over, and finally I vetoed the idea of any more swimming.

Sharks were always near the boat. Most of them were small, it is true, but they were always in evidence, and I could never be sure that a large one was not somewhere about. I have heard many arguments pro and con as to whether a shark would attack a human being in the water, but I did not feel that we should take chances. Later we were to get mighty convincing evidence, in several instances, that they are dynamite, and not to be trifled with.

CHAPTER · SEVEN

ANOTHER night passed with tiresome sameness, and the third morning found us thinking intensely of breakfast.

"When I look at that sunrise," Tony said, nodding at a rather spectacular dawn, "all I can think of is a fried egg."

It seems strange to me now that we were still not terribly worried about our chances of eventually coming out of this. When we fell into this adventure we were all in exceptionally good health, and that, I think, was why we were able, these first few days, to keep a cheerful discipline on our minds.

Our minds were optimistic, but our stomachs were not. We were good and hungry. Then it began again—the favorite conversation of yesterday, and the day before, and the days to come.

"When I get back to Missouri," Gene said, "I'm gonna

make me the biggest ham an' cheese sandwich ever seen in Sikeston."

"Ham an' cheese, toasted," Tony added.

Gene and Tony again discussed the relative merits of ham and cheese sandwiches of all possible varieties, for most of an hour.

I finally joined the conversation to get the subject away from ham and cheese sandwiches—and onto some other kind of food, for I was as bad as they.

"Someday you'll have to come down to my ranch at La Mesa," I said, "and Tony can cook anything he wants the first day, Gene can have the kitchen the second day and cook anything he wants, and then on the third day I'll take over and cook all my favorite dishes."

This was a novel idea. Gene and Tony seized upon it at once, and the three of us worried it like starving hounds, suggestions tumbling over each other.

Tony entertained us with detailed description of a full-course Polish dinner, taking us through the minutest preparation for the entire menu, to the last pinch of spice.

Gene took us from breakfast through dinner on a Missouri farm, and when my turn came I was not outdone.

Thus we plotted nine days of progressive gorging, three days at each of our houses. We really intended to do this. It was the first of a series of little compacts we made, most of them having to do with eating.

Such was about the level of our conversation, interspersed frequently with prolonged and repetitious discussion of our plight and our possibilities for rescue. From time to time one of us would offer bits of his life history, and that led into various conversational pathways, but mostly we talked of food.

On this third day I discovered that I had a pencil. It suddenly burst upon me that this was a marvelous tool. I could make a chart!

My eyes darted about the boat. Draw it on the gunwale? No, a life jacket!

I had lost my life jacket shortly after the sinking of the plane. It leaked, wouldn't hold air, so I had just let it go in the water. But we had two left, and I seized one.

I knew the approximate position where we went into the water, and long ago, aboard ship, I had memorized the positions of all the islands in this section of the Pacific. I would have to use dead reckoning, but the small celluloid aerial navigator's calculator that I had kept gave me an excellent mileage scale for my purposes.

Navigation was a fabulous mystery to Gene and Tony. They watched with great interest as I traced the lines of latitude and longitude on the front of the life jacket, and marked with tiny ovals the approximate spot where we had landed, and my estimate of our positions in the past days' drifting.

"There's where we are, and there's where we're going," I said enthusiastically. They nodded, excited but not understanding this abstruse science.

Each afternoon just before sundown I would estimate the component direction and distance of our progress in the preceding twenty-four hours, and enter it on our chart. At the same time I would make one straight mark on the gunwale to denote one more day passed. I reckoned each day to begin and end at 7:30 in the evening, which was the approximate hour that we went into the sea.

We were all so anxious to work our way westward that I would always unconsciously fudge a little to the west of the position I really judged us to occupy. The result was that in the end our plotted position was about 150 miles to the west of our true position.

Nevertheless, I was able to keep rather accurate track of our progress in this way, and the mere keeping of a chart, on which we could actually trace where we were going on the changeless sea, gave us something tangible on which to pin our hopes.

The boys were quite proud of our possessing so useful and encouraging a tool as a chart. Our daily progress meant something when you could see it drawn each evening in a pencil line. It gave us something new to talk about through the long third night.

"Well, we know where we've been," Tony said, "but where are we going next?"

That worried me too.

We had drifted south and slightly east for two days. The raft responded delicately to the wind's touch, sometimes cutting along as if we actually had canvas up, even leaving a stubby wake at times. This was most satisfactory when we were going in the right direction, but there's no controlling the winds. We could conceivably be driven in vast circles, far from the narrow shipping lanes, until our rubber-and-cloth ship rotted. When this happened, I judged, we would long since have become three white skeletons.

Thirsty, tired, and hungry, I was wrestling for a way out of this grim conclusion that had begun to nag me almost as badly as the sun itself, when a contrary breeze whipped spray into my eyes. The bow of the raft tilted upward. Then the stern lifted until it was higher than the bow, and our floor of fabric shivered.

Tony, trying to rest in the bottom, yelled as a sharp wavetop caught him in the mouth. Aldrich, white-faced, had a death grip on the stern thwart.

The boat whirled in a cloud of clear green spray, hurling me down on top of Tony. Another wave struck the port side with a stunning boom, and white water drenched us. There was no time to think as the tiny boat spun into a cavernous dark trough. Up we shot again, and then, as if a giant had smoothed the wild tumult, we were scudding swiftly but quietly before a steady southwest wind.

I dug my hands into my eyes, wiping out the stinging sea water. I looked about with some trepidation, and was surprised to find that there were no black storm clouds overhead. We were bumping along, seeming to hop from wave to wave, in a fairly choppy sea, but that was all.

That was our introduction to the swift wind changes of these latitudes. The powerful gust had treated our little inflated cockleshell as the wind treats a sail when it jibes, throwing loose booms with cannon speed. It was something to know.

We were very anxious to work westward from our starting position, and now this new wind was driving us north and east, exactly the opposite of our desires. If we were to go on like this, I admitted secretly, the outlook was not promising. A good stiff wind in the wrong direction could push this 40-pound boat—

Then I had it! Why wouldn't it be feasible to rig some sort of sea anchor to check our progress when the wind was wrong?

I immediately began to look around for some practicable means of working out my idea.

"Gimme that life jacket," I ordered Gene.

The half-inch manila rope life line still encircled the boat. I removed it, and tied one end to the deflated life jacket, the other to the gas inductor manifold on the pointed bow of the boat. The line was about 22 feet long. I cast out the jacket to see how she would work as a sea anchor.

As the jacket sank in the sea and the boat pulled to the end of her tether, the tiny craft jerked, slowed, and swung about lazily, pointing her bow into the wind.

Perfect!

We had a good line, and the jacket was just heavy enough to sink eight or ten feet in the water in fairly light wind, four to six feet in a heavy wind. In fact, the wind had to be terrifically heavy—which it was a time or two—to draw the jacket to the surface and collapse it. This happened in blows that I estimated to be 30 knots or over, but we didn't have a lot of wind of that force.

Under average conditions this improvised sea anchor cut our rate of drift to practically zero. I estimated our drift, with the sea anchor rigged, to be not more than one knot with 16 knots of wind. It held the bow of the boat directly into the wind, thus materially reducing the area of boat offered to the wind's driving force, while at the same time the jury anchor exerted its drag. These two factors combined most satisfactorily.

Now we felt quite heartened, and more the masters of our fate. A thousand disasters could still happen to us, and food and water were still as unattainable as the stars, but at least we had conquered one serious problem. We all felt more fit to tackle the others.

Tony, who had been the most despondent, perked up as soon as he discovered that I could now control our little boat. He began to take as great an interest in our progress as any of us.

This same day the wind shifted around to the north again, and in a few hours veered to the east. It seemed that the winds were most variable in this area. Our chart shows that we spent the first few days describing circles, as I had feared.

We were beginning to notice a dryness of our tongues and throats. There was no moisture coming from our salivary glands, and a withered feeling in our mouths made it hard to swallow. We had all taken great quantities of salt water in our first plunge into the ocean when the plane sank from under us. We had been afraid at first that swallowing this salt water would immediately cause us to suffer unbearable thirst, but we did not find this to be true. Perhaps, in this particular instance, this early lack of adverse reaction to salt water was due to the fact that our systems were able to assimilate immediately the mineral content of the ocean we had consumed.

Nevertheless, though we were not yet suffering greatly from thirst, we knew our systems must be craving water, and we were worried.

There were great areas of sea open to our view. Here and there, far off yet seemingly near, we could see gray and silver streaks between the waves and the darker clouds just above.

Rain.

At numerous points we could make out what we believed to be line squalls, rains along the line of wind change, or cold fronts. Many times we thought one of those squalls would surely hit us and we could get a drink, and many times we seemed to sail right between two showers. But the sun still shone on us.

The night arrived surprisingly as always in this latitude.

We watched the great red sun sink in silence. The sea this evening was dappled with tiny gold-tipped surface waves on which a bird occasionally lighted as if coming home. We felt lonely.

The tiny topmost yellow sliver of sun hung a second, then dropped, and suddenly it was twilight. Behind us, a star gleamed.

"Well, Henry," Tony said promptly, "time to put on the pot."

Why that phrase didn't get under our skins after its five hundredth repetition is one of the minor wonders of the voyage.

In the gray morning of the fifth day we realized, fully and definitely, that our force had left us behind.

Tony said it: "They aren't coming back, fellas."

This time I couldn't think of anything to say. My eyes checked every inch of the little boat from habit. Gene, on watch, was sitting on the forward thwart, tirelessly scanning the sea as it unfolded in the rising daylight.

He looked at each of us without expression, swallowed, and stretched a grin.

"Well, shucks, ours ain't the only ship on the ocean."

He turned his sharp blue eyes back to their patient vigil.

This brought Tony's volatile spirits up again.

"Some convoy—why, hell—"

We chewed this over awhile.

Shortly the sun went to work. Gene sighed and touched his long, tender nose. Tony automatically began flipping water onto Gene's blouse. I sat and dourly regarded the raw red circle where my wrist watch had been. This spot never tanned. It repeatedly burned to blisters, peeled, and burned again.

The rest of the morning passed in silence. Each of us was occupied with his own thoughts, and they must have been uniformly gloomy.

Over and over I took stock of our situation. In a few hours I would make the fifth pencil mark on the gunwale. Five days without food or water. Five days, the three of us crowded together in a space not much bigger than the inside of a bathtub. Five days with no sleep by night, and a pitiless torture by day, all day long, as the sun's burning rays bit viciously into our hides and boiled out the remaining moisture. Five days of turning our suffering skins, like basting fowl, to baths of stinging salt. Five days—and how many days ahead?—of nothing to keep us alive but the sinew that was now wasting from our bones.

I shook my head like a boxer who suddenly catches himself being counted out. Time to put on the pot, old boy.

"Boys," I said.

They stared at me, Gene absent-mindedly fingering his ludicrous young beard, which was stiff with salt.

"All we've got to do now," I said, trying to make my voice strong and confident, "is keep going south and west, and we'll either be picked up or run into an island. It isn't easy, but it might be worse, and if we stick together, I have a feeling we're going to come out all right."

"Let's shake on it," Gene said.

So we shook hands all around, and things seemed better after that.

Before evening, the three of us were sitting dejectedly silent. Then Gene made a suggestion.

"It might be a good idea," he said, not meeting our eyes, "to say a prayer."

We discussed this seriously. We found that we had all been reared in some religious atmosphere, but that we had all drifted away. It had been many years since I had been inside a civilian church, but I sometimes attended Sunday services held by the chaplain aboard ship, when my duties permitted and I was not going ashore.

We all concluded that a word of prayer wouldn't hurt anything.

So we sat in the steaming little cup that our boat had become, and bowed our heads beneath the cruel tropic sun. We each mumbled a few words of our own awkward choosing, calling on our God to bless our loved ones back home, over whom we were more concerned than ourselves, and asking for a little rain.

We were all quite skeptical about the possibility of any answer to our prayer.

"Well, now we done all we could," Tony said.

"Gee, give it a chance," Gene answered impatiently.

I called on my store of proverbs.

"God helps those that help themselves," I said.

"Well, come on, rain," Tony challenged. "Or maybe it ain't gonna rain no mo', no mo'."

We lifted our voices lustily at that and sang, "It Ain't Gonna Rain No Mo'," as far as we knew the words—which wasn't far—as if by our false cynicism we could put a reverse hoodoo on the elements.

At least we were all laughing again, which we hadn't done for some time.

Despite our elaborate irreverence, there was no denying that the prayer had made us feel better. Gene, who had more piety in his nature than either Tony or I, took evident satisfaction. His mind now was obviously clean of worries or self-reproaches.

For a time we made a game of flinging handfuls of salt water on each other to cool our chafing bodies, but soon in the quivering heat we again fell silent, and welcomed the evening.

That night it rained.

CHAPTER · EIGHT

IT was Tony's watch. Gene was lying in the bottom, his long legs jackknifed. I was sitting on the after thwart, vainly trying to get some rest with my head held in my hands. Tony was sprawled on the forward seat. Suddenly he straightened, so abruptly that the boat wobbled a bit, and I glanced up.

A drop of moisture hit me in the face. I was afraid to think it might be anything but a puff of spray.

"Hey!" Tony said softly. His voice was almost a whisper.

Several more drops struck my upturned face. Then they came faster, until we were being fairly pelted by large globules of water. It was rain, sure enough, and I've never smelled a thing so sweet.

In another instant it was pouring—a tropical squall.

"Grab that oar pocket!" I ordered. As I spoke I snatched up the life jacket and formed a hollow of its fabric between my hands.

The oar pocket was a separate piece of fabric, folded over and fastened to the boat with rubber cement. We had arranged that, in case of rain, Tony was to hold the pocket out horizontally and slightly folded, forming a trough probably twelve inches long and six inches wide. This, we figured, would hold a couple of cupfuls. Gene's station was at the forward thwart, which he was to double into a similar receptacle, while I had the life jacket. If we had a long shower and got more water than we could drink at once, we planned to fill the canvas water bottle with which the raft was equipped, by running water into it from our improvised troughs, held funnellike.

As soon as I had a mouthful of water collected in the cup I had formed with the life jacket, I bent and sucked it up with my mouth. Immediately I spat it out. Salty.

"You've got to rinse the salt out of the fabric!" I yelled over the wind. Every fiber in our fabric boat had its coating of salt, baked in. We scrubbed furiously with our knuckles, begrudging every drop of fresh water that we had to waste in washing.

The wind picked up to a low roar, and for perhaps five minutes we had a blinding, equatorial deluge. The boat sang with the sound of its beating on the drum-tight sides. We were ducking our heads like greedy fishing birds to suck up each precious mouthful as fast as it collected.

The rain ended as suddenly as it had begun, and then we lapped up what was not too brackish in the bottom of the boat.

Our mouths were refreshed and cool again. I have never tasted a better drink. And it gave our clothes and bodies a needed cleansing of five days' rime.

The small drink we had was not enough to do our dehydrated systems much good, but for that night it quenched our thirst. Unfortunately, there was none for the bottle. We hoped the next shower would not be so long in coming.

That night the wind shifted to the north and slightly east again, so we hauled in the sea anchor.

All of the sixth day we kept watching and hoping for another squall. Our thirst, whetted by that first drink, had now become intense. The water we had taken must have been absorbed almost immediately by our tortured systems. As the sun's rays heated us we had again the burning dryness in our throats that had become all too familiar—but now it was worse.

As for hunger—our shrunken stomachs were numb now.

That evening Gene suggested another prayer, pointing out that we hadn't done so badly on the first one. This time we began with hymns, "When the Roll Is Called up Yonder" and "The Little Brown Church in the Wildwood," filling in where we had forgotten the words. Then, the prayer for rain having worked so well, we decided to ask for food, and incidentally a little more rain.

After our prayer meeting we felt much better, and we talked until well into the night. Each of us told his life history, and we began to get really well acquainted.

This night I might have slept a little, I don't know. Several times I fell into a doze, and immediately, it seemed, I snapped awake with the terrifying feeling that the boat had been punctured and was sinking. This nightmare recurred several times. Other times I dreamed that the sun was cooking me, and steam was rising from my body. The other lads experienced exactly the same thing. They complained frequently about nightmares, especially later on. This was probably a result of the mental strain we were all suffering. At any rate, these nightmares added considerably to the misery of our nights. They were the more discomfiting because there was nothing we could do about them.

We were not so glad to see the dawn, this seventh morning. The sun had become our enemy.

Today there were swarms of little tropical fish swimming about the boat, feeding and playing. They would swim up close, roll on their sides and gaze at us with their little goggle-eyes, giving a very humorous effect. Actually, they were not looking at us, but at the bright orange boat. One little black fellow came within six inches of the side of the boat, and lay almost motionless near the surface of the water.

Gene, who was fishing with the knife now since our line and red-bandanna bait had failed, made a desperate jab at the little black one, but succeeded only in grazing his side. We noted that this particular fish stayed with us about three weeks. We could distinguish him after that by the white scar left in his dark hide by Gene's knife.

Everything we had of metal was rusting badly by now, especially the gun, which was a better grade of steel than the pocketknife and useless pliers. Frequent salt-water baths began to rust the gun's blue surface, which was a thin coating of oxidization. The inside of the barrel also was rusting, but occasional shooting at birds kept this part clean, at first. When the inevitable corrosion began to set in, Tony made every effort to keep the gun in good condition.

Every day after the sun had dried the boat and everything in it, Tony would go to work on the gun, scraping and cleaning as best he could with no oil. We had a little grease from the inside of the empty magazine clip, which we had taken apart to see what useful pieces we could get out of it. This grease was too heavy to be of any real benefit, but Tony used all of it on the pistol, in an effort to keep it in working condition as long as possible. The grease helped some in keeping salt water from the magazine slide, in the grooves and working parts, but there wasn't enough.

The pocketknife and pliers we scraped and polished as best we could.

GENE ALDRICH was the most patient fisherman I've ever seen. I was not very enthusiastic when he announced he was going to try to stab a fish with the pocketknife. I figured it would occupy his mind and provide some amusement, anyway, so I made no objection.

He would lean out over the boat, poised and ready. Whenever a fish, near the surface, would venture too close to the edge of the boat, Gene would swing down with the knife, but the wise little creatures were too agile.

Tony, meanwhile, was lying in the bottom of the boat, dozing.

I was watching Gene's maneuvers warily. If the boat got punctured, we would indeed be in a bad way.

One fish, about the size of a fresh-water perch—the kind we used to call a "punkin perch"—was especially curious. He kept swimming up close, slipping over on his side, and gazing out of one eye at the strange yellow thing, our boat.

Then he came a little too close.

Gene stabbed viciously.

His knife caught the fish right amidships, the blade going almost completely through.

Gene whipped the fish into the boat with one continuous motion of his arm.

The fish fell from his knife and dropped on Tony.

That brought Tony out of his dozing in a hurry.

Quick as a cat, he rolled over on top of the little fish. He doubled his arms close to his chest, and pressed his body down like a football player on top of a fumbled ball.

Tony lay on the fish until it stopped struggling.

When he was sure it was dead, he lifted it by the tail, holding it gingerly and well into the center of the boat, so there would be no possibility of our losing.

"Chow!" he said reverently.

"Come on, lemme scale it," Gene said, reaching out his hand.

He took the fish, and laid it carefully on the forward thwart.

With the knife he scraped off the scales, working carefully and thoroughly. Then he handed the knife to me.

"You divide it, chief."

I cut the fish into three equal pieces.

"I never ate raw fish before," Gene said, a little squeamishly.

"Well, the Hawaiians eat raw fish," I answered.

"Don't worry, I'll eat it," he declared.

Each of us gnawed off a small bite. We had no saliva in our mouths, and trying to masticate the raw flesh was like chewing gum.

The moist innards went down a little better.

"The liver's good for you," I said, and divided this organ among us.

We ate as much as we could of this fish, but it was poor fare for our first meal in seven days. None of us had ever tasted raw flesh before, and in spite of our long fast we were wary of it. The dryness of our mouths and throats made it extremely difficult to swallow.

We didn't want to eat it all at once, anyway.

After we had eaten as much as we could, there was a sizable portion left. This I wrapped in one of the rags I had torn from Tony's shirt. I stored it in the bow of the boat.

"There's a meal for later," I said.

This was our lucky day.

That afternoon it rained again.

Our method of catching water hadn't been too successful the first time. We didn't really get enough for our needs, and I had been casting about in my mind for a better scheme.

I hit upon the idea of soaking the rain water up in rags. I made the boys take off their underdrawers, and I took mine off too. I cut them along the inside seams, making of each pair one rag about thirty inches long by fourteen inches wide.

These worked quite satisfactorily. The drawers were of absorbent cotton material, and seemed to pick up the water as fast as it came down. In the beginning we used the shirt rags too.

We could see this second squall coming. The rain came up very fast, especially the last hundred feet; then it seemed to hit us all at once.

This time we were prepared. The boys made a trough of the oar pocket and I wrung out the rags as fast as I could. When we had sufficient water we formed the oar pocket into a little run-off, and thus poured the water into the water bottle. This water bottle was a baglike receptacle that closed with a zipper. It had been put in the boat as a bailer, but we had a better use for it.

The squall was a short one. In this part of the South Pacific squalls never last longer than fifteen minutes at the most. Normally they last from three to five minutes, but they hit with a bang and the water falls in sheets so thick you can see only a few yards.

Our rags were always heavily impregnated with salt, and before they could do us any good as water catchers we had to rinse them out. Often, before we had them freshened the squall would be gone.

There was always a lot of wind in the squalls. One seemed to bring the other. The wind was very sharp, whipping up quick surface waves that would ride over the ground swells, and often the squalls brought a reversal of wind, or a wind that crossed the previous direction. This condition always made nasty little waves that jumped in the air and plopped in the boat, sometimes throwing a couple of gallons of salt water over our water-catching rags. This meant that we would have to rinse them again, losing precious time in the brief shower.

This time, however, we all had a good drink. This, on top of our first food, made us feel very much better.

After the rain had passed, we took off all our clothes. We sloshed the sodden garments in the bottom of the boat, soaking up the excess water which was useless for drinking because it was saltier, from washing the brine-coated fabric, than the sea itself. We wrung our clothes over the side, and put them on again, refreshed.

The rain had washed the atmosphere as well as us. It was late afternoon and the sun's rays were softer. There was a good breeze from northeast by north. All hands felt better than at any time since the first day.

It was Gene's watch, so I chased Tony from the bottom of the boat, where he was dozing again, and lay down myself to try to get some rest.

I had been lying on my back for perhaps a half hour, my eyes closed, when there was a terrific explosion.

I came out of the bottom of the boat like a streak of lightning. My ears were ringing; in fact, I haven't been able to hear again out of my right ear to this day.

But I hadn't time to think of my roaring eardrum then.

Gene had shot an albatross.

The bird had alighted on the stern of the boat about six inches above my head.

Gene was sitting on the forward thwart, facing aft. This put him about five feet from the bird.

Slowly, his eyes fastened on the albatross, he reached down and picked up the gun.

Gripping the .45 in both hands, he aimed carefully, and fired.

The blast went directly across my face. The muzzle of the gun was hardly an inch from my ear.

The slug caught Mr. Albatross in the center of the breast, and plowed the length of his body. The bullet missed his heart, but scrambled his innards some.

The impact knocked the big bird several feet into the water.

These details I learned later. As I leaped up under the shock of that shattering blast, Gene and Tony were yelling:

"Get him! Get him! Don't let him get away!"

The bird's carcass was drifting slowly away from the boat, but in their excitement neither Tony nor Gene was making any move to do anything about it.

I took in the situation at a single glance. Instantly, I dived over the side.

Whether I was strong enough to swim, the possibility of my being unable to get back to the boat, never occurred to me. I struck out after the floating body of the albatross. A few strokes, and my fingers closed in his feathers.

I was back aboard before the boat had drifted twenty feet.

We tried to pluck the bird, but we found it impossible to pull out the feathers. So we skinned it with the pocketknife.

None of us was very hungry after eating the heart, liver and other organs, including the entrails. We put the rest of the meat in the bow with the fish, intending to eat it for breakfast the next morning.

Naturally, we recalled the Ancient Mariner's curse. I knew that all seamen since olden times have held the albatross in great awe, and believed it sacred.

Like the average person, perhaps, I have always been just a little inclined to believe in good luck and bad luck. I didn't think much about it at the time, but later I was none too happy over Aldrich's feat in shooting the albatross.

[71]

My watch came around at about midnight. I got up and took over. It was very dark tonight.

After sitting awhile on the after thwart, I noticed a glow of light in the bow. It was so strong that it illuminated the entire boat, and the sea around. It seemed to be coming from our pile of rags.

I got down and untangled the rags until I came upon the meat we had saved from the fish, and the carcass of the albatross. They were strongly phosphorescent, especially the bird. When I held it up, the albatross glowed like a flashlight, particularly the tail, which seemed as bright as an incandescent bulb. The fish glowed where it had lain against the bird.

I aroused the two boys.

"What do you think of that?" I said.

We gazed at the stuff for a moment or two, not wishing to make the decision that we knew we must.

"Looks like it's spoiled, all right," Tony said slowly.

Gene came right to the point.

"I don't know about you fellas," he said, "but I wouldn't feel like eating any more of that."

"What makes that?" Tony asked.

I explained phosphorescence, and pointed out that phosphorus was poison.

"It might be dangerous to eat any more of it," I concluded reluctantly.

"Damn albatross poisoned the fish too," Tony said.

The fish meat emitted a soft green light only where it had lain against the albatross.

"Yeah, better heave it all," Gene said, looking down.

Without further talk I threw the whole mess into the sea.

Later it occurred to me that I should have saved it for bait. As a matter of fact, I found out later that it wouldn't have been dangerous to eat the albatross, at all. The flesh of an albatross is phosphorescent as a rule, I learned, because it preys largely upon luminous fish.

The rest of the night passed uneventfully, until just before daylight, when the wind shifted to the west. I rigged the sea anchor. In about an hour the wind changed again, shifting back to almost due north, and I took the anchor back in, and we continued on our way south.

As soon as the sun was up, Gene had out the knife and was trying to stab another fish. Our stomachs had been stimulated by the few bites we had, and now the hunger began to claw the walls of our bellies with red-hot fingers.

AFTER destroying all our food supply, we were worried about getting some more. Until those meager bites of fish and bird gave our stomachs something to work on, we hadn't known what real hunger meant. Today, we learned.

Evidently yesterday's few mouthfuls started our digestive juices to working. I began to think that I had read somewhere that when the stomach was left empty for a long time, these acids would begin to work on the walls of the organs themselves, so that one would literally be digesting his own insides. This idea persisted in my mind. It was most disquieting.

Being the eldest and captain, I felt it my duty to keep to myself any thoughts that might lower the morale of the boys, though it was hard to deny myself the common solace of sharing my misgivings.

This was the eighth morning. We were making fair time, on nothing—the nearest islands were hundreds of

miles to the south, by my reckoning, but we were heading in their direction. There were weary, plodding
leagues to go, but if the wind was kind we would get
there—we, or what was left of us.

Physically we were not in bad shape at all, yet. We
were coasting, as it were, on the stamina we had started
with, thanks to the hard regimen of the man-o'-wars-
man. Our faces were drawn, under the beards and flecks
of shedded skin, but our muscles were still hard despite
our almost entire lack of exercise. My orders were strict
that no unnecessary movement must be made, to save
the fabric of the boat from friction wear. We couldn't
swim for fear of sharks, which were thicker about the
boat every morning.

We could see their black fins in the water everywhere.
We watched them lie in wait, then rush and close their
long jaws on luckless lesser fish that played innocently
about the raft.

Some of the smaller fish would hide beneath the boat
when these voracious monsters came near, but there
were always plenty who failed to escape. It was an ab-
sorbing drama, this life of the sea. It was cold and cruel,
and we were part of it now.

Gene, for a while this morning, studied the play that
was going on around us. Then he conceived the idea of
trying to stab a shark.

There was a group of small sharks preying around
the boat, now and then snapping at the gay little fel-

lows that ventured from their sanctuary underneath. There were five or six sharks darting all around us. They were about four feet long, and yellowish brown in color. They looked like sand sharks.

As the morning wore on and the sharks became more familiar with the boat, they grew bolder.

Gene was leaning intently over the side, his knife held ready, dagger fashion.

Finally, a shark swam bravely up to him.

The knife flashed out and down, and there was a sound like a punch.

Gene turned pale.

"I—I think I hit the boat," he said. He held his hand in the water where he had struck.

There was a quick, convulsive thrash and Gene's arm was yanked like a line.

"Wait! I got him," he yelled.

He had been fortunate enough to strike the shark in the gill. That, we learned later, was the only spot vulnerable to the little knife.

Quickly, but with care, Gene hauled the shark into the boat, using the knife like a hook.

Tony again was dozing in the bottom of the boat. The shark landed right on top of him.

I haven't had the experience yet of having a live shark, wet and bleeding, thump me in the ribs while I was half asleep. It nearly scared the wits out of Tony.

The yelp of surprise was hardly out of Tony's mouth,

though, when he grasped the whole situation. Like a wrestler, Tony flipped over and slammed all his weight on the struggling sea beast. He concentrated every ounce of his energy on holding down the sinewy, slippery thing.

In about ten minutes the shark lay still. Tony slipped off carefully, on deadly guard, ready to pounce again if the shark so much as quivered.

"Okay, let's cut him," he said, after catching his breath.

The shark's hide was rough as sandpaper. Examining it closely, I discerned a pattern of small circles on his skin, that looked like scales but weren't. It resembled linoleum.

I tried to cut him, but his hide was too tough. It was like working on cured leather with a butter knife.

"Hold his head, Gene," I suggested. "Tony, you better sit on his tail. Looks like this is gonna be a job."

With both my hands free, I took a firm double grip on the knife and bored with the point.

Finally, after considerable exertion, I got a small cut started. Then I jammed the knife in to the hilt. Using both hands, I pulled toward me as if I were hauling on a saw handle, and thus I managed to split the length of his belly.

"Where are those pliers?" I said. "We'll skin the devil."

Easier said than done.

[77]

With all our ingenuity and patience, we found it impossible to skin the shark with the tools we had.

I gave up skinning, and cut out his liver. I recalled reading somewhere that sharks' livers store up vitamins, so I thought we'd better eat that first, before something happened to it.

The liver was quite large. I cut it into three equal piece, and we devoured it before exploring the shark's possibilities any further. We had eaten just enough fish the day before to stimulate our appetites, and we were consumed by hunger at this time.

After getting the raw liver down, I looked into the shark's stomach. There were two herring there, one whole and one bitten in two at about the center of the body.

"Aldrich caught the shark, so he ought to have the whole one for himself," I proposed. Tony assented.

Gene, delighted, ate his fish happily, and Tony and I feasted on the other which had been fairly divided for us by the shark.

I have never in my life tasted better fish than that was. The herring must have been worked a little already by the shark's digestive juices, for it tasted as if it had been cooked.

This was a royal banquet. We ate all the other organs that appeared at all edible, which was everything that we could chew into condition for swallowing.

Then we started taking the meat from inside the skin.

It was not a case of cutting this leathery flesh, but of tearing it, viciously, from the anchoring tissue.

We ate perhaps two-thirds of the meat at this one sitting. None of us had a mind to deny ourselves a good bellyful. The meat was tough, and had a peculiar flavor, sort of an ammonia taste. It was not at all pleasant or palatable. It tasted like—well, like shark, if you've ever imagined how a shark would taste. It was not like any fish I had ever had before.

When we had eaten our fill of meat, we held up the tail and head, forming a pocket in the center of the carcass in which a large quantity of blood collected. The blood was thin and watery and strong-flavored, but we downed it manfully, every drop.

I would not care for shark meat as a steady diet.

The sun was very hot today. I was afraid the remainder of the meat would be too badly spoiled to eat by the next day, but we put it away in the bow of the boat, thinking that if we couldn't get another meal out of it, we could use it as fish bait—if we could devise some sort of hook.

With our stomachs full for the first time, we felt pretty good.

Tony slapped his sun-tanned belly contentedly. Food had reawakened his optimism.

"How far we gotta go to make an island, chief?" he asked.

"About five hundred miles, south," I calculated.

The wind was bearing out of the northeast now, and I thought things were going rather well. Some of the larger islands, I figured today, were near our path. I can't name the specific islands we wanted to make; we're under the secrecy of war. However, there are a number of archipelagoes in the South Pacific. There were various possibilities of coming upon friendly land. I hoped to reach one of the larger islands, which I knew had coconuts on them. Some other islands did not.

Along about here I began to worry about enemy submarines. I wondered what we would do in case we sighted a submarine in the daytime. I decided that if we saw a sub we shouldn't take a chance on its being of our own forces. Instead we would deflate the boat far enough so that it would flatten in the water, and make ourselves as unnoticeable as possible.

If this step became necessary, we planned to inflate the boat, after the submarine had passed, by lung power, since we had no pump. We realized the serious peril of taking this risk, but we had to decide the alternatives.

The chances were good, I thought, that if we did sight a submarine, it would be an enemy. I knew that if it should be an enemy sub and they spotted us, they would probably pick us up.

Three American sailors in these waters would be a prize. We would certainly be questioned. I didn't know what that would entail for us, and I firmly shut my imaginings.

Then, I figured, the chances were good that after they questioned us, they would do away with us in one or another of several ways.

Certainly they wouldn't care to take us on the submarine, haul us back to base, and put us in prison.

I decided then that rather than take a chance on a sub, we would take a chance on an island.

CHAPTER · ELEVEN

WE had another prayer meeting that night, and every night thereafter. Each evening, after the sun's flamboyant departure left us feeling more alone in a world that suddenly lost all color, we devoted perhaps an hour to our informal service. There was a comfort in passing our burden to Someone bigger than we in this empty vastness. Further, the common devotion drew us together, since it seemed that we no longer depended entirely upon each other, but could appeal, simultaneously, to a Fourth that we three held equally in reverence.

After our halting prayers—neither Gene nor I was scholarly in formal religion, and Tony could pray only in Polish—we developed naturally the "fellowship period" familiar to those who have attended Protestant Sunday school.

We sang some popular songs, a time or two. I couldn't remember any except old ones. I hadn't been to a dance, except occasionally, in twelve or fifteen years, and popular songs go away from me. The songs that I knew, the boys had never heard. The more recent ones that they could sing, I couldn't. However, we managed to get together on a few, and that gave us a lift.

It was later that I came to realize how little we knew about the Bible. One night, after our prayer meeting, I told a little Bible story. Appropriately, it was the miracle of the loaves and fishes.

The boys were tickled with it. In my youth I had been brought up in a denomination of the church that holds regular Sunday school, so I drew upon a long memory. Of course, the stories were in my own improvised words. I hadn't been to church for many years, so it's easy to imagine how good I was at recalling the stories I had learned as a youngster. I hadn't been inside a civilian church since 1923, when I was back home after my first cruise. Aboard ship, the chapel services which I occasionally attended included everything but Bible stories.

My religious training had been such that I could now recall all the favorite stories of the Scriptures, but nowhere near verbatim. Gene recalled a number of stories, but couldn't tell them. He would think of a story, and then it would be up to me to tell it.

Tony had never heard any of these things before. In his church, all the services were in Polish—or Latin. The best-known Biblical tales were all new to him. He begged me every night to tell him more and more.

Well, I didn't want to tell him everything I knew in one night, so each evening I'd tell one story. That went on until the end.

I found my recollections of the Bible very useful in the last week or ten days, when we were all exhibiting a tendency to brood over our position. One of my hazy parables would snap us out of our depression and start a flood of discussion in which our dismal outlook was momentarily forgotten.

Many a time I wished a preacher, or someone well versed in Scripture, were present. The wording I used would certainly shock a Bible student.

Nightfall brought a quieting in the boat, such is the force of lifelong habit. The night was cooler, and more treacherous, and when the moon was down and clouds covered the stars, it had a darkness that few landsmen know. Sundown brought a lull in conversation. The prayer meeting gave us a sense of having an evening, but then our lids grew heavy, and we remembered bitterly that somewhere folks were crawling into bed.

In such reflections we fell silent, each of us with his own thoughts, which I imagine came close to a pattern.

Gene took the watch. Tony lay down in the bottom again and tried to sleep. I idly checked the constella-

Tony Pastula, Harold Dixon, and Gene Aldrich after they had been "fattened up" for a few days following their escape from the sea. *Official U.S. Navy Photograph*

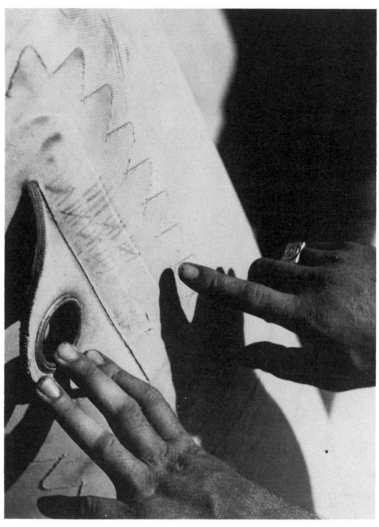

The marks on the fabric of their raft by which Dixon kept count of their days at sea. *Official U.S. Navy Photograph*

Aldrich, Pastula, and Dixon in Honolulu after their recuperation was almost complete. *Press Association, Inc.*

Robert Trumbull, city editor of the Honolulu *Advertiser* and correspondent of *The New York Times* in the uniform issued by the U.S. Army to newspapermen in Hawaii. *Official U.S. Navy Photograph*

There was not much room to spare on the raft. *Press Association, Inc.*

Admiral Chester W. Nimitz, commander in chief of the Pacific Fleet, presents a commendation to Aldrich aboard a ship at Pearl Harbor. Behind Aldrich stand Pastula (left), who was also commended, and Dixon, who received the Navy Cross. *Official U.S. Navy Photograph*

The raft itself, as it now appears on display at the United States
Naval Academy Museum. *Official U.S. Navy Photograph*

tions, and tried to keep my thoughts impersonal by going over and over various navigational calculations regarding our position and probable drift.

We sat thus for some time, our thoughts accompanied by the monotonous lapping of small waves against the raft. Several times a sense of something changed, somehow, tried to disturb my reverie. Finally, moved by some automatic sense, I looked up, and discovered that the stars had disappeared. At the same time, I noted a subtle difference in the atmosphere.

Then I became conscious of a growing sound—soft, like the wind rustling palm fronds, but with a higher tempo, and steadier. In another few seconds the first big drops hit my head and shoulders, and I immediately roused Tony.

We were having another rain.

Our arrangements for catching water, once rehearsed, were like a well-drilled manual. The shower thudded upon us with violent fury, then was as quickly gone. Our system of making every pliable inch of fabric into a vessel, augmenting the water thus caught by wringing out the highly absorbent rags from our shorts, gave us all a good drink this time.

When the brief rain was over we again disrobed and wrung our clothes. To us, this was almost like having a bath. The refreshment braced us mentally, and we chatted fairly merrily for perhaps an hour until the heavy night began to press again and stilled us.

The wind had lightened when Gene's second watch came around.

"Don't seem as if we're moving," he said as he settled on the forward thwart.

"Hard to tell," I agreed sleepily. I was wishing for a bunk.

Gene wet his finger and held it up to test the wind.

"Ain't hardly no breeze at all," he said.

He leaned over the side and dipped his hand in the water, to see if he could feel any drift.

His fingers had no sooner got into the water than he let out an agonized yell. Instantly, as if he had touched something scalding hot, he whipped his arm upward, high.

A gray shape flung itself from his hand and went into the water on the opposite side of the boat, with such a splash that a small spray plopped back into the raft.

Gene was holding his wrist by the other hand, and was moaning softly.

"My God, what's the matter?" I asked.

"I think a shark bit me," he said.

Tony was up now.

"Jeez, is it bleeding?" he asked, deeply concerned.

"Yes," Gene said.

It was obvious that Gene was badly frightened, as indeed we all were.

In the darkness we could not see how badly he was bleeding. Of course, under the circumstances Gene believed his injury was worse than it actually was—and it was bad enough, indeed, to cause concern.

Fortunately, I had a handkerchief. We bound his fingers, and the bleeding soon subsided.

It was plain that Gene had been badly bitten by something. We agreed that it must have been a shark.

I was impatient for the first light of dawn so I could examine the finger closely. When morning finally arrived, we saw that the wound had bled surprisingly little, considering the severity of the cuts.

The hand was badly lacerated. Tooth marks showed plainly on the fingers. The shark—if shark it was—had raked down his index finger, cutting almost completely through the nail in two places. The root of the nail was so thoroughly mangled that it was plain he would lose the entire nail eventually.

I began to realize how badly we needed some sort of medical kit.

CHAPTER · TWELVE

T HE experience of almost losing his hand in a shark's mouth took all the starch out of Aldrich for a while, but we tried our best to cheer him up. And so the hours wore away.

By morning we were all very hungry again.

Remembering the spoiled albatross and tainted fish, we had some misgivings when we hauled out the remainder of our shark meat for breakfast. However, it did not smell too bad, so we tasted a bit.

It was better than it had been the day before, fresh from the sea. The sun had almost cooked it, and the meat was somewhat dehydrated by the heat. Also, it had been drenched frequently by salt water, and dried by the sun each time, which seemed to remove some of the ammonialike flavor.

We ate all the meat this morning that we could tear from the skin and bones. The lower, or tail, section was so tough that we could wrest little from it to chew, but we had better luck from the middle part and the head. All of this we devoured.

What we found inedible in the shark at this meal we used for fish bait. All our attempts to fashion hooks from the shark's bones failed as utterly as had our plans to fashion barbs from parts of the gun. There was anything but a lack of patience in our efforts, but in the end we had to abandon, regretfully, the whole idea of catching our fish in the traditional way, on a line.

The shark meat seemed to act as a purgative for Gene and me. In all our time in the raft—nine days now— none of us had had a bowel movement, although our kidneys functioned normally. Today, as a result of our first good meal of the voyage, Gene and I had normal action. Incidentally, this was the only one; we were not to be allowed another.

Tony was not so fortunate. He complained for several days about stomach cramps, but could not achieve a movement. Finally, about a week later, he managed a passage, and after that he felt much better.

Nine days of continuous exposure had not yet hardened our skins against the sun's fierce rays. Our beards, long and unkempt by now, protected our faces partially, I suppose, but our lips and tender noses continued to suffer. They burned raw, peeled, and painfully burned again. The round patch on my wrist, where I had worn a watch for many years, felt as if it had been seared by a branding iron. Most of the time this spot was covered by a heavy scab, until the scab fell off, and it blistered and scabbed again, and again and again.

We had a lot of trouble with our lips, especially Tony. Stinging salt-water baths, which we could not avoid, continually irritated the cracked and blistered flesh.

When sea water splashed in Tony's face, he could not refrain from licking the brine from his lips with his tongue. Then he would bite them in his pain, and start them bleeding. My own lips were split and cracked from sun and salt, but I was careful not to bite them or irritate them in any way, and they would heal—later to split again, of course.

Tony's never healed once, and bled throughout the voyage.

The heat gradually increased as we worked southward. February and March are the midsummer months in south latitude, and also the rainy season, so we hoped for increasingly frequent showers so we could save some water against a nonrainy day.

The wind varied somewhat as we entered the second week. At times we would have to put out the sea anchor to check adverse drift, but usually this would be for only a few hours at a time. Generally, the wind bore from the north-northwest. During these days we averaged about forty miles a day going south and slightly east.

The marking of the chart at sundown became, like

the prayer meeting, a ceremony that was eagerly awaited in the deadly, hot monotony of our days. Any small activity, any new thing to talk about, relieved the growing mental tension. At times the rubber tub seemed to press in upon us, as the need for space to stretch our aching limbs became a torture. Not even in a chain gang, I think, have three men been confined so close together for so long. There was rarely a time that two of us, at least, were not in actual contact with some part of our bodies. When we were all sitting up at the same time we could perch away from each other on the inflated sides, but even this was as if the three of us were sitting on the edge of a flower pot with our feet rooted together.

Our dispositions were beginning to show the strain. So far we were maintaining a careful affability in our relations with each other, but polite answers were beginning to come more slowly, and with obvious effort. Our inability to sleep, or even relax comfortably, was having this result.

So our minds were greedy for any diversion. The boys watched with great interest as I fiddled with the little celluloid mileage scale, figured mentally, and finally drew my deliberate marking for the day on the jacket-chart. Then, with all the dramatic timing I could muster, I added another pencil scratch to the growing calendar on the gunwale. Another day, another thirty or forty miles.

The boys discussed our progress with me, and asked a lot of questions. I explained the whole process, and Gene and Tony listened raptly. Neither of them knew a thing about navigation, so at their suggestion I began giving them elementary instruction.

They had no idea of direction. Neither one could tell north, east, south, or west from the sun, moon, or stars.

I explained that early in the morning, when the sun rose in the east, there was a good chance to get our reckoning, and that when the sun set in the evening it was going to set fairly nearly due west.

At night, I demonstrated that the stars were an excellent source of direction. I used principally Polaris, the Southern Cross, and various prominent constellations as they progressed from east to west.

I worked with the boys night after night, and eventually they grasped enough so that I could trust them, when they were on watch, to keep fairly close track of our direction. Then I would lie down and try again to sleep—a nightly battle between me and Morpheus, which I always lost.

My efforts did not make navigators of the boys, and I was just as glad, as this left the responsibility for our progress entirely in my hands.

Meanwhile Gene's injured finger was beginning to swell, with dark blood pressing under the nail. It was not infected, however, and was showing all the signs of healing nicely. I attributed this to the action of the salt water. The area around the nail was very painful, though, so I took the pocketknife and drilled a hole in the nail with the point, to relieve the pressure.

It was obvious that Gene would bear for many weeks the scars of his encounter with the shark.

I happened to mention this once.

"Well, it's a romantic scar, anyway," Tony laughed. "Imagine being able to say, 'That? Oh, that's where the shark bit me!'"

"Yeah, you'll get a lot of fun out of that, Gene," I said.

"If I live," he drawled, grinning.

CHAPTER · THIRTEEN

ON the tenth, eleventh, and twelfth days we had almost continual squalls. At last we filled our water bottle, which held enough to keep our throats wet sparingly for a day or two. After this mean ration was safely stored, we found that the blessing of rain could turn into a curse. We had no means of saving more water than the little rubber bag would hold. The rest that fell was worse than wasted, for we had to bail it out of the boat. Worst of all were the tricky waves that squalls brought. These bounding hillocks of sea water kept dumping heavily into the raft. Thus the weather we had prayed for now became a threat to our lives.

We had no implement for bailing. However, we did an adequate if not satisfactory job by taking off all our clothes, sopping up the water in the boat, and then wringing our dripping garments over the side. During this operation we were continually in each other's way, which added no little to our irritation.

Time after time we would no sooner get the boat free of water than a high green comber would curl down upon us, half filling the boat with churning foam and pushing down the side on which it hit until I thought we would surely capsize. But the boat always rebounded with a sickening rock to the opposite direction, sending our cargo of sea water whirling about our knees as if it had been given one violent stir with a giant whipping spoon.

The danger of losing our footing in the overpowering tumult and plunging into the writhing sea struck us with a dread that seemed to stop the blood in our veins.

We exchanged no words at these times, but alternately held and bailed. It was as well; we could not have heard each other in the threshing tempest.

Here we had the feeling, for the first time, of being hand-to-hand against the sea. There was no time to think of hunger; that gnawing pain was now becoming part of us, and we paid it heed only when there was no more immediate worry on our minds. Right now we were fighting a physical, bruising battle for our lives.

The almost constant bailing, added to the considerable exertion required merely to keep ourselves inside the heaving raft, was drawing heavily upon our waning strength. I feared the storms were using the energy and stamina that was all we had to live on.

When the last lashing rain left our boat behind, it was with great relief that we fell against the thwarts exhausted, and lifted our haggard faces to the sun.

On the twelfth day the sea was still rough, with the choppy surface showing whitecaps as far as I could see. During my watch in the morning I sat on the forward thwart, scanning the glaring blue water for anything that might affect us, the while noting ruefully that my sunburned face, which had been relieved in the cloudy days, was growing hot again.

Suddenly, well ahead, I saw something strange bobbing in the water. I tried to see it again, but it had gone behind a wave. In a moment it reappeared. It looked brownish.

We were bearing down upon the object, and I stood up to watch more closely.

As we drew nearer, I saw that it looked like the nose of a seal.

That's strange, I thought. What in the world is a seal doing in this place?

I was familiar with seals, having watched them off the West Coast many a time. I thought it was odd that I should encounter one in this far latitude.

Well, I mused, we live and learn.

The closer we approached, the more the thing began to look like a seal. I couldn't think of anything else.

The round, brown thing obviously was not a fish;

although it bobbed, it kept more or less the same position in the water.

I thought perhaps the seal was afraid of some large, predatory sea denizen, and was coming up frequently for air as it watched its enemy.

In a moment we were abreast.

Then I was puzzled again.

If this is a seal, I thought, it should be frightened by the boat. Why doesn't it dive or swim away?

Suddenly something flashed in my mind.

I whipped around, looked hard, and half rose, then sat down again and cursed.

I turned to Gene.

"See that thing way out there?" I asked, pointing.

His eyes picked it up.

"Yeah," he said slowly. "What is it?"

"Does it look like a seal?" I asked.

Tony was in on the game by now.

"Seals don't belong down here," he declared.

"If it ain't a seal, what is it?" Gene demanded, having convinced himself by now.

"Well, maybe it could have got away from home," Tony admitted.

Having gained my support now, I put an end to it.

"Well," I said, "listen. If there was room in this boat, I'd let you kick me for a damn fool. That was no seal, fellas! Damn it! It was a coconut!"

That left them with their mouths open.

I have never in my life felt more provoked at myself. And I had never felt so hungry, as I reflected bitterly that I had as good as thrown a heaven-sent meal in the ash can.

"Aw, hell, don't take it so hard, chief," Tony said. "Where there's one there's others."

"Sure, chief," Gene said. "There's more where that came from."

After that we kept a coconut watch—made it part of the lookout's job.

Tony had had no chance to clean the gun during our three-day rain, and it had now deteriorated very badly. The gun was wet continually from rain and sea, and the salt water particularly had speeded corrosion. When dry weather came again, Tony went to work at once. He chipped off thick rust and polished the corroded parts as best he could, but the automatic mechanism was beyond repair. The gun would no longer reload itself.

He got it working after a fashion, however. We could put one slug in the barrel, force the slide back to the lock position, and fire one round. Then we had to pull out the empty cartridge by hand, and shove another in —a tricky and laborious process, and worrisome since we could see that we were soon to lose our pitiful armament, such as it was.

The gun was in this condition when I shot the shark.

CHAPTER · FOURTEEN

EARLY in the morning of the fourteenth day there were many small sharks playing around the boat. They were between three and four feet long, with an occasional big one that ran to six or seven feet. Obviously they were after the small fish which clustered about us constantly now, feeding on the moss which had begun to grow on the bottom of the raft. At this time there were about a dozen of these beautifully colored tropical species swimming about, now and then disappearing beneath us in their search for food.

Gene was vigilant with his knife, trying to repeat his feat of gilling one. Sometimes when Gene became tired I took the knife, and several times I came pretty close to getting one of the sharks, but I was more optimistic of spearing a smaller fish. They came within reach frequently as they made for the food growing on the raft's bottom.

Then a leopard shark, about seven feet long, cruised up and frightened all the smaller sharks away. He seemed more interested in the boat than in his natural prey. He slid around the boat several times, about a hundred feet away, with his dorsal fin sailing high out of the water. After he looked us over a while, he swept directly under the boat, diving to about two feet beneath the surface. If I had had the pistol I could have shot him as he returned slowly, at a speed of three or four knots.

I was not pleased at his scaring those prospective meals away—the smaller sharks and fish. I thought I had better chase him off.

"Tony," I said, "hand me the gun."

Pistol ready, I waited. I figured that the leopard shark would go around the boat, and try swimming under us again. Sure enough, he passed under the boat, swung out about twenty yards, circled around to the leeward side, and headed straight in toward the boat again, as before.

I threw the pistol off "safe," and got ready, not moving for fear of scaring him as he moved in. This time he did not sound, but approached smoothly and deliberately, straight down the wake of the boat. He almost stopped when his head was directly below my pointed pistol. The muzzle was only about four inches above his forehead. Quickly centering my aim, I pulled the trigger.

It had never occurred to me that I might be firing

too close to the water. When I pulled the trigger, water shot up like steam and threw my hand about two feet in the air. The blast almost blew the gun from my hand, but somehow I managed to maintain my grip. The muzzle's being so close to the surface blew a fine shower into the air from the powder charge, and it was a second or two before I could see what had happened to the shark.

When things cleared away, he was down about ten feet, spinning around and down like a corkscrew. He was sounding as rapidly as he could, and these sharks have tremendous power. He was gaining momentum at every twist of his sinewy body. Evidently I had wounded him mortally; I never saw him again. I had hoped to kill him, but I learned later that a shark's brain is more toward his nose than I had aimed. I probably broke his spinal column.

In a very short space there was a whole pack of sharks around. I assumed that they had already polished off their wounded fellow, and were looking for further prey, as they did each morning and evening when the fish were feeding.

We were disappointed at having killed fair game and yet being unable to claim it for a meal. About this time we were beginning to notice a deterioration in our physical condition. All of us were losing weight rapidly now. We were long, wiry types—I was the heaviest, weighing about 180 pounds when we started. So far, however, we had borne up very well, but now our experience was about to take its toll, that was plain.

We were not downhearted, yet. With each passing day we felt our chances were better of being rescued by a convoy; we knew that many of them must be passing through these waters. Of course, when war broke out our vessels were forced to swing wide of the regular trade routes, because the Japs were in possession of the Marshalls and other groups of islands in that area. At that particular time the enemy was just about sitting astraddle of the beaten path to the Orient through this way.

We also knew that we were rapidly approaching the more southerly groups of islands, where our chances of making a landfall would be good. However, the particular stretch of sea that we were crossing now was almost entirely devoid of islands, I knew. Rescue by a convoy would be luck, we realized; our best chance was still to keep working southward, holding on to life until we hit an island, whenever and wherever that might be.

Aldrich's earlier success in catching fish spurred his efforts now. Hour after hour he leaned over the side of the boat, stabbing at every swimming creature that came anywhere near his reach. He made many attempts, and though he was unsuccessful, his patience never gave out.

On this fourteenth day he was rewarded. A small specimen, exactly like the first, got a little too near the boat, and Gene's long brown arm sprung out like a snake's tongue. He drew it back triumphantly with the fish impaled on the knife in his hand.

Our hunger had been very intense the four or five days after eating the shark, but was now beginning to subside—a dangerous sign, I thought. We had been getting drinking water fairly regularly, thanks to the squalls, so we were able to eat this fish with relish—and, I might add, without delay.

Aldrich, throughout the rest of the day, redoubled his efforts to land another fish, but without success. He put away the knife regretfully when darkness fell.

That night it rained again. The comforts and discomforts brought by rain had become routine. We didn't talk so often now, but went about our duties automatically as circumstances called. The shower tonight was fairly heavy. We had our drink, then bailed by our cumbersome sop-and-wring method until the boat was empty. The shower over, we wrung out our clothes and hauled them on again, with little comment. We were getting tired.

A few minutes after the shower ended I lay down in the bottom of the boat to try again to rest. I closed my eyes, although it was very dark. Suddenly I became conscious of a scratching noise on the stern of the boat, just above my head.

I opened my eyes to see what was causing the noise. It was a bird, calmly perched there.

Neither Gene nor Tony appeared to be aware of our

visitor. Very carefully and noiselessly I slid my hand up inside and as close to the edge of the boat as I could without taking a chance of causing some slight scraping sound on the fabric.

Then I quickly grabbed, and had him by the leg.

The flapping and squawking and general commotion that immediately ensued brought the boys to my assistance. Gene and Tony whooped in their excitement, but were as careful and methodical in their movement as I was as I concentrated every bit of my brain and body on holding onto that bird.

In a moment Gene and Tony held it securely. Gene took his knife, grasped the bird by the beak and face, and efficiently cut off its head with a deft stroke.

It was a small bird.

"Ain't another albatross, is it?" Tony asked. We were all feeling about its feathers in the darkness.

"Naw, too small," Gene said.

"Well, I'm afraid it's too dark to do anything with it until morning," I said.

"Better let me stow it away in the bow," Gene advised.

Stow it he did, amidst a clamor of speculation and delight. There was more conversation that night than we had had in several days, as we impatiently awaited the morning.

We examined the bird in the gray light before dawn. It was a young tern of some sort.

We picked off his feathers, and proceeded to eat. The

little fish of the previous day had reawakened our dormant appetites, and we were ravenous.

The tern's flesh was tender. To me, it tasted like dried chicken. Of course, by now we were over any squeamishness we had felt, at the start, about eating raw flesh.

CHAPTER FIFTEEN

"HEY, we must be near land, chief."

It was Tony who spoke suddenly. With food in his stomach and plenty of water, Tony had become a livelier member of our crew. He was taking a healthy interest in our progress now.

"Near land? What do you mean, Tony?" I asked.

"Look at that junk," he said, sweeping his hand around to indicate the gentle swells that rose and fell about us in regular motion, like a sleeper's breast.

Bits of debris floated on the hot, blue waves, wet sticks glinting.

From my calculations, which I was keeping with care, I judged that we still had far to go, but the presence of driftwood was at least a hopeful sign.

"That stuff floats a long way—it can go clear to the Coast," I said. I preferred to be pessimistic today.

"Well, we never saw any before," Gene argued.

"That's right," I admitted. I was deliberately letting

the boys think they were swinging me to their own viewpoint. It helped their morale.

Suddenly, I took more interest.

"Say, some of that stuff may be useful," I said. "Keep a sharp lookout on that debris for anything we can use!"

It occurred to me that my mind must be getting dull in the heat and hunger and confinement, or I should have thought of this the minute Tony called my attention to the driftwood. In fact, I was a little irritated that I had not seen it first.

Tony and Gene talked volubly between themselves, pointing to this and that bit of material floating out of reach, speculating on what it might be, and where it came from.

I merely sat, stewing miserably in the equatorial sun. It was becoming hotter every day as we moved southward. The relentless heat, intensified by the glaring water, was sapping our strength. There was no escape from this heat, this burning light that struck our eyeballs from whichever direction we turned. And the salt was itching in my beard.

As my watch came on I stirred and wet my hands in the sea to wash my face. Rising and taking my position on the forward thwart, I stretched and flexed my limbs, which now were cramped a great deal of the time in our tiny space.

"Put your head in the bottom and you can get some shade," I told the boys.

Trying thus to take advantage of a few inches of shade was like drinking from a stream whose banks are just too high to let you lean down and suck up water without falling in. We decided it wasn't worth the trouble.

Finally, we caught something from the flotsam close to the raft that looked as if it might be useful. It was a piece of coconut stem that obviously had been cut and used as a paddle by some South Sea island native. He had evidently taken it from its parent tree with a machete, whacked it off cleanly with one blow. It was about three feet long, and made a very passable canoe paddle.

Such an implement would have been very welcome to us in the calms that were to come, but this one had been in the water too long. It was rotten, and too far gone to be of service to us. We tried to use it, but a few strokes broke it. However, we kept it for any possibilities it might offer in the future. We finally lost it when we tipped over.

"Wonder where that was used?" Gene pondered.

The coconut stem paddle at least gave us meat for hopeful speculation. It was comforting to come upon evidence of human life in this waste.

As we progressed to the south and east, down through this area, we saw many new varieties of birds and fish, leading us to believe that we were nearer some reefs, at least, where shallow water made good breeding grounds for the fish. Reefs always furnish excellent feeding for fish and marine birds. When these appear in such abundance as we encountered now, it is a pretty good indication of reefs. As practically all the reefs in the South Pacific bulge up into small islands, we had hopes of sighting land at almost any time.

"Suppose we do hit an island—might be a desert island," Tony suggested.

"A desert island would be better than no island at all," Gene answered him.

We discussed the possibilities, and devised a plan.

What we had in mind, in case we reached a small island, was to stop over on it, feeding on the eggs from nesting birds which were sure to be plentiful, shellfish, and such other fare as the island might offer. Then, when our strength was restored and we were back to normal, we would stock the raft as well as we could and push on, south and west, with the first favorable winds.

Of course, right from the beginning our ultimate goal was an inhabited island of one of the larger groups to the south. With this end in view, it was our constant endeavor to husband our all too meager supply of tools and clothing, and to maintain our fragile boat in the best condition possible. For this reason I kept constantly examining the fabric for worn spots, and touching up those I found with sparing use of our rubber cement.

As the fish became more plentiful we were learning the facts of marine life. Several varieties of large fish soon appeared, preying on the smaller ones, which seemed drawn to our raft. The big fellows would leap clear of the water in their voracious dashes at the smaller fry, which also jumped wildly in their frantic endeavor to get away.

This performance always caused a lot of excitement and conjecture among us. We were always hoping that one of the smaller fish, which seemed to leap blindly away from their pursuers, would drop into the boat. But none ever did, and we were unable to catch another with the knife.

We were not too far engrossed in our own suffering to appreciate the teeming sea life about us. On calm evenings, about sundown, sometimes the entire surface of the ocean as far as we could see would be one seething mass of small fish. They tumbled about each other almost as thick as sardines in a seine. The flat, windless water, green and smooth as bottle glass in the fleeting moments just after sunset, would literally roar with their frantic churning as a large fish made his rush from the depths and jumped high in the air. The instant the big fish's body cleared the surface of the water on his upward surge, the small fry would calm down until they saw another big one coming.

One variety of the large fish always ran three and four in a pack. They were built like bass, and looked as if they weighed seventy-five to a hundred pounds each. They leaped four to six feet out of the water, usually coming out at an angle of about 45 degrees. The small fish were not so terribly agitated by these as they were by the one that was shaped like a torpedo. This vicious creature was about four feet long, and weighed perhaps sixty pounds. He had a pretty blue stripe down his side, which only accentuated his murderous appearance. His powerful lunge shot him out of the water almost vertically, and sometimes he ascended to a height which I estimated to be thirty feet. When one of these was jumping, the small fish were in the greatest fear, and made the water boil as they ran for their lives. At these times the sharks gathered around in droves to look for wounded fish. They seemed to get a great many. The powerful leaper appeared either to capture or wound a fish on nearly every run.

We saw one school of large porpoises. They came up and played around the boat a few minutes, then were off. We never saw them again.

The birds had a circus when schools of minnows surfaced. There were several varieties of birds, but the most plentiful were the terns and the white bird with three long feathers in his tail. This beautiful little fellow was a diver. He would get up quite high, and shoot straight down at his prey. He seemed quite independent, associating only with his mate, while the other varieties liked to gather in flocks for company.

All these birds, except the albatross, were very evidently afraid of the larger fish. They never remained on

the surface of the water longer than a second or so—
in fact, they stayed on the waves just long enough to
grab a minnow and take off again.

Always after a long, hard rain the birds were obviously exhausted. They had to exert themselves to the
utmost to stay in the air until their feathers dried and
relieved them of the weight of water. At these times
many of them attempted to land on our boat to rest,
but invariably were frightened off by the sight of men.
As they flapped away in laborious flight, their chirrup-
ing was pitiful.

By far the most majestic of all—and, like the shark,
entirely unafraid—as he wheeled and circled in unend-
ing turns and dives, was the mighty albatross. He is the
undisputed monarch of the air.

Like all seafaring men, I have paid some attention to
the superstitions of my trade. Many times as I watched
this lordly bird I recalled the Ancient Mariner's curse,
and the despairing line, "With my crossbow I shot the
albatross." I still waited for the second one to come,
but so far the albatrosses that approached our boat were
impersonal in their relations with us.

This regal voyager of the air has an enormous wingspread. He is built like a soaring glider, which he emu-
lates in his flight. In a fairly high wind he hardly ever
moves his wings, but takes advantage of the upcurrents
from the big swells to sustain him. His graceful movements and almost unbelievable agility in maneuvering

were a never-ending source of pleasure to an aviator such as I. I sometimes expected to see him fall off into a spin, but his sensitivity to the point of equilibrium was so great that he could merely slide a shade from one wing, go into a short slip and pick up speed again in a few feet, thus avoiding what looked like a sure crash into the water.

The more the albatross impressed me with his aerial magic as I watched him, the more I came to appreciate the qualities the Ancient Mariner must have seen in the bird to hold him sacred.

It was the next day that we encountered the fateful "second albatross" I had been half expecting.

CHAPTER · SIXTEEN

W E passed the night of our fourteenth day, and entered our third week with a dead calm. It was one of those times in the South Seas when all nature seems to stop for breath. The air becomes oppressive, and the heat, unrelieved by the soothing trade winds, suddenly acquires weight and presses on you. Humidity rises, and the perspiration will not evaporate from your skin.

In the utter lack of breeze the sea was flat and viscous. Even the birds were listless; only the fish were free of the torpor that descended over the world of air breathers.

Without wind, the rubber raft was motionless, like the famous painted ship upon a painted ocean—I recalled the line.

Most of the sea birds had left us in the night, but still following our boat was an old gray albatross of huge wingspread. He came circling about the boat, seeming to inspect us for a long while from a distance of about a hundred yards. Finally, as if he had decided something, he banked steeply and shot straight in toward the boat. He landed on the water close by, and calmly gazed about him like a hoary old doyen. He did not show the least fear of us, but began unconcernedly dunking his head in the water, occasionally giving us a casual sidewise glance.

Eventually he had maneuvered himself to within ten or twelve feet of the boat. Then he stretched out his long neck and poked his head into the water as deep as he could. He kept his head submerged for several seconds; he was evidently feeding on something, but I could not see what it was. I noticed that he had white feathers in the roots of his mottled tail. After several minutes he took off and flew directly westward.

I had taken in this whole show from start to finish, and somehow felt much better after it was all over. I hoped we would soon have favorable winds.

That was the first time I had seen the great gray albatross, but not the last. The next day he was back again, and almost every day thereafter. Sometimes he was in company with a black one. Perhaps I was becoming too imaginative, but the appearance of the gray albatross always impressed me uncomfortably. Later events convinced me that this was indeed a bird of evil omen.

As a result of the recent rains, our pistol now was rusted beyond repair. Previously I had been able to insert a shell by hand and force the gun closed, in this way firing one round at a time, but rust and corrosion finally won. The gun had rusted so badly during the days when we were unable to clean it, because of continuous rain, that it had become almost one solid piece of metal. Tony, by exerting all his strength, was able to remove parts that we thought we might be able to use in improvising fish spears or some other implement to arm us if we should land on an uninhabited island. He then drew out the barrel, with a hard struggle, to make as great a length as possible of barrel and frame. We left the gun in this position to rust solid, thus making a passable hammer. This, we figured, would come in handy for breaking open shellfish, coconuts, or other edibles that we might be fortunate enough to find on an island.

Our pliers and pocketknife, our most useful tools, were not so severely affected by corrosion as was the gun, which was a better grade of steel.

That night we talked some about our plight, which was growing worse every minute that we were without favorable wind. Sundown brought a little comfort, but it was not cool—it was less hot.

The fifteenth day dawned on a torpid sea. As the morning wore on and I saw no signs of the calm lifting, I began to wish we had some means of rowing. Our strength was a little less with each foodless day, and I felt it necessary that we should make some sort of progress. Besides, rowing would give us something to do. Hour after hour we had gazed at the sluggish sea from our reddening eyes, seldom speaking, seldom smiling. Activity might be a tonic to our dulling spirits.

I looked over our stock of gear for some means of improvising oars. The inventory didn't take long. Finally my eyes lit upon my shoes, which I was still saving. I studied them thoughtfully; the only possibility was there.

"Gene," I said, "give me the knife."

He turned his head slowly, after a moment, without interest.

"Give me the knife," I repeated.

He handed it to me, and turned back to his contemplation of the silent sea.

My shoes had thick, live rubber soles, and low heels. With the knife I cut away the uppers of one shoe, slicing off the leather flush around the heels, but leaving about a half-inch of the uppers attached around the toe. This formed a sort of cup, and was also to act as reinforcement to keep the sole from bending backward under pressure of the water.

When the upper part was carved away to my satisfaction, I drilled a hole in one side of the instep. I passed the shoestring through this hole, evened up the ends of the cord and tied it down with a square knot. I then tied another square knot in the joined outer ends of the strings. This formed a permanent loop that could be passed about the wrist of the rower, so that if he inadvertently dropped the shoe it would not be lost.

After finishing the first shoe, I moved over to the forward thwart, sat down and tried it out.

"Glory be!" I whispered.

My scheme was going to work.

I could dip the shoe into the water and, pushing backward, create a perceptible forward drive. It worked exactly like a small canoe paddle, except that my arm was the handle.

In a few minutes I had made another "paddle" from the other shoe, and thus I created our motive power.

"Look alive, lads," I shouted, elated with accomplishment. "We're going places."

When the boys saw that my idea would work, their listlessness vanished. This new control over the raft that we had achieved was like a weapon placed in the hands of a fallen man.

"Let's get agoin'," Gene said, enthusiastic now.

I believe it was Gene and I who started. Gene was on the starboard side and I on the port. In fifteen minutes we had stretched a wake behind us.

"You rest now, Gene," I said. "Your turn, Tony."

Gene moved back to the stern to rest. I slid over to his place, Tony took my former position at port and rowed with a will. After fifteen more minutes, as nearly as we could judge, I went aft for my rest, Tony moved to starboard and Gene came in at port.

Thus we spelled each other, circling counterclockwise. All that day we rowed, never stopping, until about two o'clock the next morning—almost eighteen hours.

As I had hoped, action raised our spirits. We chatted gaily, and even tried a chantey or two. We exchanged all the lore we had on the art of rowing—or paddling, as you will. Sometimes the man resting in the stern acted as coxswain, counting the stroke and calling hilariously for "ten big ones for deah old Hahvahd!"

Fifteen minutes' rest for each man as he finished his half-hour shift kept us fresh; shifting from one side to the other every fifteen minutes kept us from straining either arm. At that, it was rather tiring without food to sustain our strength. A sparing swig of warm water from the diminishing supply in the little rubber bag was welcome refreshment.

At about two o'clock in the morning a breeze sprang up from the east, driving us on in the direction we had been rowing all day and night. We were quite fatigued by now, and were elated that the suddenly risen wind should keep sending us in exactly the direction we wanted to go.

We "shipped oars" gratefully, and composed ourselves to rest as best we could for the remainder of the night. The exercise had quickened our minds as well as our blood, and we were quite optimistic as to our chances of reaching one of the larger islands that we knew to be off to the westward.

Before closing my eyes to try to doze, I checked our progress by the stars. We had rowed a hundred miles.

The next day, however, we lost all that we had gained.

CHAPTER · SEVENTEEN

THE winds turned variable and shifted us about, sending our little boat skidding for a few hours in one direction, then likely as not it would turn on the opposite tack and make an equal distance the other way. It was irritating to be losing time in this way, for each passing hour that we were not heading the way we wanted to go was in the most literal sense an hour taken away from our lives.

Finally a steady breeze held in the northwest. This was worse, for it drove us back eastward about a hundred miles, the same distance that we had so laboriously paddled to the west. This contrary wind worked us about fifty miles to the south as well. We were becoming discouraged, when another flat calm descended. We took up our shoe paddles and rowed back westward for eight hours straight before the wind set in from the east, and took us westward again.

Now I discovered how I had unconsciously miscalculated my position on our chart, in my anxiety to work westward. About this time we passed through the spot where I thought a large inhabited island should be. Actually, we were about a hundred miles east of this island, I learned later. The fallibility of my chart was a setback. I tried to console myself with the reflection that such an error was to be expected under the circumstances, especially since I had no navigation instruments except the little mileage scale. Nevertheless, finding that I couldn't tell exactly where I was gave me a disquieting feeling. I didn't communicate my disappointment to the boys, but concentrated, rather, on buoying up my own confidence.

"Dixon," I said to myself, "if *you* get discouraged—" I didn't finish the thought, but resolutely put it out of my mind and turned to our immediate concerns.

The raft was still in good condition. Our gear was holding up well—what was left of it—except that the water-catching rags were becoming frayed. The two lads had lost their socks, and their feet were painfully sunburned. My own socks were full of holes and almost rotting from the sun and salt water, but still gave my feet some protection.

Of us three, Gene Aldrich suffered the most from sunburn, partly as a result of his own stubbornness, or carelessness, in not heeding my advice to keep rags about his head. I frequently advised both the boys to keep their heads covered as well as they could against the sun, but

Gene preferred to let himself burn. As a consequence, he was always suffering, and complained incessantly. His nose and face, particularly, burned and peeled time after time. He just couldn't tan. With his fiery red face and thin fringe of youthful beard, he looked like one of those spider monkeys I used to laugh at in the zoo. I sympathized with his pain, but he was the funniest-looking human being I have ever seen.

Tony's darker skin tanned fairly well, so he didn't suffer so much. His lips, however, were continuing to give him trouble. I finally got him over the habit of sucking the blood out of them, as I convinced him that by doing this he was literally sucking out his own strength.

My own skin was the swarthiest of all, but much as I tanned a particularly hot day would take off my hide like scales from a baked fish. Our only relief was to bail water over each other. This was cooling, but the salt on our raw red skin caused hours of torment.

For the first time now I became conscious of bodily weakness. That first long, hard session of rowing left us all fagged for three days. We were just beginning to regain our strength when we again took up the paddles for eight straight hours. After that we were never so strong as before. We lost flesh rapidly from this time onward. It was not long before our bones were sticking out like red-glazed knobs.

The sun was beginning to have its effect on our minds

too. I noticed this first in myself as a shortness of temper. I became annoyed at the boys over little things that I wouldn't have noticed had I been normal.

I became particularly irritated at Gene. I would ask him a question, or tell him to do something, and instead of answering me he would continue to stare straight ahead, as if he had not heard. It was impossible to tell whether he was lost in thought, or was just slipping into a doze. Then I would fly into a violent rage, and scream at him. After a minute or two of this I would stop to catch my failing breath, and usually some little sound like the lapping of a wave against the raft, or the forlorn squawk of a sea bird, would recall me to my senses. At first I apologized to Gene for my unreasoned outburst, but when I saw that he was not listening I lapsed into morose silence myself.

Eventually Gene would snap out of his trance, and become talkative, but his conversation wandered. He would begin an anecdote, and before he had completed his thought he would be on a different subject. When I considered Gene's condition during my own lucid moments, it occurred to me that the strangest phase of his behavior was the fact that he sometimes was the sanest of us all. His spells of absent-mindedness came intermittently and without warning. As I look back, I see that my own reaction to the starvation, thirst, confinement, and heat was no less unreasonable. One moment I would be solicitous and concerned for the boys;

without warning my mood would give way to blind anger. At such times I couldn't understand why they did not jump to obey the instant I gave an order. Then I would curse irrationally, as one swears at a stone after he has stubbed his toe on it.

Tony's reactions came to be about the same as mine. Until about the third week he was terribly despondent; after that, his stanch nature came to life.

Tony had a heritage of warm blood; as privation began to work on him, as it did on us all, he showed it in shortness of temper. Sometimes, when we all happened to be in a jolly mood at the same time, I jokingly congratulated him on the vocabulary he could show when his ire was aroused. Tony would grin at this, a little sheepishly. Ordinarily, he had a sweet, shy nature that shrank from violence either of action or of language.

"Well, I never liked to fight when I was a kid," Tony explained once. "But one time a fella got me cornered and I guess I beat the hell out of him."

I reflected that it was good to have these lads along. They were young, they were inexperienced with the sea, which had been my profession for twenty-two years. They were just two American boys, neither with any extraordinary advantages. One was from a farm, the other was the son of an immigrant. They joined the colors to fight a war which neither had any particular equipment for, and one day they found themselves up in the air, hunting submarines with a tough old chief petty officer. And now here they were, three weeks in a little rubber float that turned them like birds on a spit beneath a flame every rainless day. In that time, the food and water we put into our bellies would hardly have sustained, for the same length of time, the poor creatures we had eaten. Still, beside me here, they were stubbornly fighting off a death that must become more certain and more horrible every day that we avoided it. No one yet had suggested the easy way out. If anyone thought of it, he didn't let on.

"Back in Missouri," Gene said, "the peach trees bloom swell."

"I wonder how Irene's getting along," Tony mused.

Irene was Tony's girl, back in Youngstown. They planned to marry, when the war was over and Tony was out of the navy.

I considered briefly the topics before the house, peach trees in Missouri and Tony's girl in Youngstown. I decided that I would rather hear about anything other than peaches. We had had Missouri peaches for breakfast, lunch, and dinner for a week now.

"She sounds like a pretty intelligent girl, Tony," I said.

"Yeah—she works for a doctor now, and she's anxious to get into some kind of war work—Red Cross or something like that."

So we talked about Irene for a while, and indeed she

must be a fine girl. Later Tony showed me some of the poetry she wrote.

Gene was on watch, and not taking much part in the conversation since I had dodged his favorite subject. I was sitting in the bottom of the boat; Tony was lying down. It was getting to be about that time of day when the equatorial sun seemed to take on a positive malevolence, drying up our spirits and making the mere effort of talking an exertion to be avoided if possible.

Suddenly Tony sat up.

"I feel a coconut," he said.

Gene and I watched him, stupidly. "I feel a coconut" —the statement didn't make sense. Was Tony imagining things?

"Didn't you hear me? I felt a coconut bump me under the bottom of the boat."

That was different!

I jumped up and looked over the side. Sure enough, there was a coconut bobbing just out of reach in the water.

"Get it!" Gene said.

The water-soaked shell looked slick, so I didn't try to grab it. Instead, I dived over the side, caught the nut, and heaved it back into the raft. The boys put the nut down carefully, and helped me back aboard.

"I felt something bump me on the back, see," Tony said, elated, "and the first thing I thought of was a coconut!"

The thick, fibrous outer husk had begun to rot—evidently the coconut had been in water a long time. However, the shell was still intact; it acted as a float, and at the same time kept most of the salt water from the nut itself, which reposed snugly within.

Soaked as it was, the outer shell was easy to remove. I pulled it off, a strip at a time, with the pliers. Then I took a piece of metal from the defunct pistol, and punched a hole in the eye. First I tasted the milk inside, to see if it was fit to drink. It was a little brackish, but not too bad.

I passed the nut around, and each of us took a turn until the milk was all gone. Warm and brackish as it was, the drink was refreshing after our long diet of nothing.

After we drank the milk we cracked the nut open and divided it. The meat made a fairly substantial meal, by our easy standards.

It was particularly fortunate that we had come upon a coconut, for our systems needed oil. Twenty-one days in the sun of the tropics had boiled the moisture from our bodies, and our skins were dry as parchment. I felt as if I had been flayed.

CHAPTER · EIGHTEEN

WHEN I unrolled our little piece of patching material to see if it might make a sunshade, I found a small pair of scissors.

They were about four inches long, blunt-ended—dime-store stuff, meant for cutting patches. Wrapped in the fabric, they had been protected from the salt water that had ruined our gun. But they weren't much good anyway.

"Might come in handy sometime, but I don't know how," I remarked to Tony.

He glanced at them apathetically. He raised his hand to brush his long hair out of his eyes, an automatic gesture, and that suddenly gave him an idea.

"How about a haircut?" he suggested.

"Yeah," Gene said. "It might be cooler."

I looked at their tangled mats of hair, and fingered my own, doubtfully. I didn't think these cheap scissors would make much headway. We had no combs, and our hair was continually falling down over our eyes. It was one of those small annoyances that sometimes bother a man more than much greater things.

"Want me to try it on you?" I asked Tony.

"Sure, come on," he said.

Tony's hair was as stiff as a shaving brush. I sawed away above his forehead, cutting close. When I ended he was a funny-looking object. He didn't have much beard, just a thin mustache and a few tufts on the end of his chin, which gave him the look of a caricature Mongolian. Gene's beard might be called the scattered type. I cut his hair too, and then Tony cut mine. The scissors weren't much good for this sort of thing, but at least these crude operations got the hair out of our eyes.

We were keeping a sharp watch for coconuts, but we weren't seeing any. We saw a lot of small, brownish nuts about two inches long and perhaps an inch and a half in diameter, that looked like miniature coconuts.

"Take a paddle on the starboard side, Gene," I said. "We'll row over and get one of those things."

Gene and I, with the shoes on our hands, maneuvered the boat to where I could lean out and pick up one of the nuts. We managed to break one open, but there was nothing fit to eat inside. They weren't nuts at all in the real sense of the word, but just a lot of fiber around a hard core. I think they were the little cones that grow on what the Hawaiians call the hala tree, which is the same as the pandanus.

"Shows we're near land, anyway," I said. None of us missed the slightest opportunity to feed our optimism. We really believed we were sure to come upon an island, and kept an untiring watch on the horizon for the blue shadow that would be land. Several times we were almost fooled by low cloud banks. I reasoned, finally, that the type of island we should reach in this vicinity would most likely be pretty flat, whereas the kind that look from a great distance like clouds would be the mountainous type that was far out of our reach to the north.

On the twenty-second day, as I recall, we found the log. Time was beginning to run together for us now. One long, blazing day was exactly like another, which makes it difficult to place exactly the small events that interrupted our monotonous routine.

We saw the log as a large, dark object that bobbed in the water about a hundred yards away. We had been brooding along, not saying much and hardly thinking. It was too hot. Until the sun went low, late in the afternoon, we did little that we didn't have to do. Hours would go by without a word being spoken. There was little one could say that hadn't been said already too many times.

Tony spied the log, and pointed.

"Look," he said.

I noted idly that his voice was hoarsening.

With some effort, I pushed myself erect by my arms and peered where Tony pointed. Gene, on his knees, leaned on his chest against the gunwale and looked too, shading his eyes with both hands.

Tony picked up a shoe, I took the other, and we swung the raft about. With long, labored strokes we paddled, and caught up to the drifting log. It was the whole rotten stump of a tree. I held the raft away from it until I saw that it had no sharp broken-off limbs or other protuberances that might injure the raft.

"It's no good," Gene said.

"Wait!" I said. "Looks like it's got some shellfish or something."

The three of us examined the stump closely, and found a lot of tiny shellfish of some sort clinging in the decaying crevices. They were very small, and resembled clams. They were too minuscule to break open, so we picked them off and popped them into our mouths like berries, chewing them shell and all.

I found a couple of tiny crabs, and gobbled them whole. I also discovered two tiny oysters—perhaps an eighth of an ounce of meat.

There was no food value to any of the stuff, although I suppose we got a little calcium from the shells of the minute clams, which were soft and easy to chew into moist powder.

Finding the log raised our spirits some. We spent a

long time picking it over for what we could find, exclaiming and comparing our discoveries. When we finally let it go, the tension of the past few days was broken, and we sang again at prayer meeting that night.

We still had the greatest faith in our ability to hold out until we reached an island, and we had not abandoned hope of being picked up by some ship of our own forces. Things hadn't got really bad up to this stage.

By now, food was almost our entire theme of conversation. Early morning, late afternoon, and night, Gene and Tony could talk for hours about the different dishes they had eaten, and their preferences as cooks. This particular topic was becoming tiresome to me, and I joined in but seldom. Most of the time I was not enthusiastic about talking, preferring just to sit and watch the waves. I began to feel as if I had been floating forever in a desert of sky and sea, adrift in a blue globe that never changed. I wondered how it would feel again to walk a broad deck. I tried to remember, and it was like reaching for the memory of a story told in childhood, or things half recollected from a dream. I thought of my wife at Calavo, and of shipmates, and of planes that I had flown. And I thought of the afterlife, and what it would be like to die.

I thought of the sea, but not as an enemy; I was unable to personalize so vast a thing. The sea was everything; it was all; it was big as—as God.

We still had water, because we rationed it by sips. In the middle of the day, when the sun was so incredibly hot that we felt as if we were chained beneath a canopy of flame, a taste of water was mighty refreshing.

We had had a strong breeze out of the west for some time. Then, on the twenty-fifth day, we again had the terrifying experience of a sudden shift of wind, this time from due west to southwest.

Noon was overtaking us when the sky began to cloud. Some distance to our left an ominously rolling mass, almost jet black, appeared in the misty gray, and for the first time we heard thunder. The sea was growing dark, and rising uneasily. The black cloud spat a thin stream of electric flame, long, thin, and forked. It darted like a snake's tongue, licking the sea. The burnt air crackled, and the sharp burst of thunder made us jump. The sound seemed to smack on every wave and surround us in diminishing leaps, and finally die unwillingly.

The powerful swells were coming faster, and dangerously high. The rising wind seemed to be blowing toward the center of the squall, and it whipped the water like an egg beater, driving swift, pointed waves crosswise into the mighty swells which now were towering above our heads. The raft was bouncing like a child's ball on a rubber string. The massive swells pushed us up and up; as they passed beneath we dropped sickeningly, bobbed in the depths of the trough, and started to rise again with frightening speed. All this time cross waves were smashing against the gunwales, sending us lurching drunkenly sidewise.

Like a great slap in the face, the rain hit. It drove down violently, in solid masses. We couldn't bail for the moment, but huddled together on one side with our backs to the wind and rain, holding the life preservers over our heads with both hands. We found, too late this time, that it didn't pay to sit together, with our weight all on one side. The lighter side was in the air; a wave struck the under edge with a loud boom! and the next instant we were in the water, the raft flying through the air over our heads.

I saw a flash of white—our rags for catching water! I let the boys look out for themselves, and made a wild grab for the rags. I got both of them, as the raft fell back and hit me on the shoulder. It was upside down.

The boys didn't have their life jackets on, but since the boat, doing a loop-the-loop, fell right on top of us, it was just a case of grabbing and holding on, while the waves beat us and blinded us and tried to pull us away.

I remember being worried about the possibility of sharks. You think of such things automatically. They run through your mind, in a way, but you don't realize this until it is all over, and the danger is past.

It was fairly easy to right the boat this time. We made the wind assist us. The raft was so light that we merely had to raise the side facing into the wind, and the wind swept under and blew it right over, just as it had done a moment ago when we were in it.

We were so concerned about getting back into the boat that I don't remember that the effort was particularly exhausting. When we did get in, however, we could do nothing for a few minutes but sit and blow, so evidently there was more exertion than we realized while we were doing it.

The full realization of our close call struck us now. Sopping wet, storm-tossed, and still being beaten by the rain as if with whips, we shook all over in the nervous reaction.

We squatted in the corners of the boat, holding on for our lives, our heads down before the fury of the storm. We had the presence of mind, though, to see that our weight was dispersed so that the raft would ride as evenly as waves and wind allowed. Thus we rode out the gale, and survived our closest brush with death to date.

When the rain stopped, we raised our dripping heads and were surprised to see that the clouds had broken, a mile or so away, and the sun was already shining through. The wind dropped instantly, and the sea, while very rough, was no longer in a terrifying frenzy. Nature's quirks are startling and dramatic in the tropics. She's like a spoiled, willful woman. Her moods change violently, and to extremes.

We stripped off our clothes and cleaned the boat of water by soaking and wringing out our shirts. Tony had no shirt, so he used his trousers. Gene couldn't wring very much, as his hand was still in bad condition from his encounter with the shark.

With our clothes wrung almost dry and freshened by the wash, we felt clean again.

"Better check the losses," I said. I was considerably worried over what might have gone in the tip-over.

I had saved both the water-catching rags. Fortunately the sea anchor happened to be tied by the line, and it was safe. The other jacket, which I was using for my chart, was lying in the bottom of the boat, but hadn't fallen out—it had got wedged into the forward part. Most of the tools were safe in the little tool pocket forward; they had been placed there just in case something like this happened. The can of patching cement also was in the tool pocket. The zippered container of fresh water was buttoned down; there was no danger of losing it. I immediately tasted the water to see if it had been ruined by the submersion. Fortunately it hadn't, although it had taken on a little more brackishness.

The only things we lost were my head rags, the remainder of Tony's shirt, and the hammer we had made from the gun.

The sun came out strong, and had just dried our

clothes when we ran into another brief squall that soaked us through again.

Tony was disgusted.

"Chief," he said, pulling off his trousers to bail and wring all over again, "it's the little things like this that annoy me."

CHAPTER NINETEEN

CALM follows the storm; we found it so. We rested. I was sore in every bone and muscle. I felt as if I had been flogged.

The sea whose fury we had felt was dreamy now, ominously so, like a tired and resting wild beast. We felt some apprehension that it might wake at any moment and claw us down again. The last encounter had left us with greatly lessened strength, and we were afraid that the next time one of us, at least, might not get back into the boat.

We lay some time, recuperating slowly. But the captain has a job to do, I thought, so I pulled myself to the forward thwart and studied our position.

Tony roused eventually, and Gene.

"Guess I'll overhaul the gear," Tony said, opening the tool pocket. While he scraped with a fingernail at flecks of rust on the knife, Gene looked about for fish, but they weren't venturesome today.

The old gray albatross was with us again. Things were getting back to normal.

"We aren't getting anywhere, boys," I said. In the still and sultry air the raft sat like a lily pad.

Gene's dunking had put some life in him. "Let's row awhile," he said. Bad hand and all, the boy had guts.

"Westward ho!" Tony said.

We rowed westward for eight hours. Then, as evening came, we again picked up an east wind, as we had before.

Our evening prayer meeting always raised Gene's hopes.

"Wonder who'll be first to see land?" he remarked.

Tony rolled over on his back and raised his knees to his chin.

"Whoever does oughta get a party," he said.

"Tell you what," I suggested. "Whoever first sights an island or a ship or something that rescues us, or is the means by which we're rescued, wins a dinner from the other two."

"Anything he wants," Gene stipulated.

"He can pick the place," Tony added.

"Hotel, night club, anything," I agreed.

"Night club—boy!" Tony said. "If I win I don't wanta collect in Honolulu. I'll take mine in Frisco."

"If I get it, it's gonna cost you guys plenty," Gene declared.

A lively discussion started. I had "been around" more

than the boys—anyway, they were younger—but none of us was a night rounder. We talked awhile about the famous night clubs we had read about in gossip columns, and each of us had a favorite restaurant somewhere. We agreed, however, that the winner had the say, and the sky was the limit.

At length talk faded, and we tried to rest.

The twenty-sixth day dawned wearily. That last eight-hour row left us weak. I know, at least, that I was never so strong again.

Today I noted with dismay that my feet and legs were growing numb.

Long days, long nights.

Our minds were growing dull. It was a physical effort to talk, and we did little of it. We shook ourselves to a brief mental awakening when I marked the calendar on the gunwale, counting the days backward one by one, and came to 27.

"Hey, boys," I called, trying to sound jovial—but I guess I wasn't even fooling myself. "It's our anniversary! We've been in the water a month—the twenty-eighth day began a minute ago!"

Tony's lips moved, but his face and eyes were without expression.

"Hurray," he whispered tonelessly.

I looked at Gene. His lips were stretched. He thought he was smiling.

Next morning sharks were about—big ones. I didn't like this very much. I was afraid one of these seven-foot monsters would rush against the boat, which might result in any of a number of misfortunes. I watched them closely and somewhat apprehensively as they circled about, their dorsal fins out of the water.

Gene would have taken the knife and tried to stab the first one that came within reach, but I discouraged this. With these big, tough babies, it would be a lucky stab indeed that caught one in a vulnerable spot, if there were any. I thought the knife was hardly big enough—it was about Boy Scout size. A hard jab against the shark's leathery hide might even break the blade, or knock the knife from Aldrich's hand. Any harm to the knife, I felt, would be a major loss. It was our only weapon now; we would have to use it carefully.

"Oughta get a meal," Gene muttered. He put the knife away and said no more about it. All Gene was willing to talk about now was food.

One big shark was cutting close to the boat. I straightened my legs painfully and leaned over the side, watching him. He looked as though he was up to some devilment, and I didn't like it at all.

The other sharks had moved some distance away, probably scouting for easier prey than us, but this one huge beast, speckled like a leopard, evidently still saw possibilities and hung around.

Finally he drifted off a few yards, turned sinuously

on the surface and with one powerful thrust of his heavy
tail shot himself straight back like a torpedo. He twisted
to a stop perhaps a foot away and seemed to look me
right in the eye, his wicked teeth showing.

I hauled off and banged him square on the nose with
my good right fist. Well, that was one surprised leopard
shark. He whirled and whipped away like a scared mon-
key. I guess he didn't come back.

Tony had seen the whole show. He reached over and
raised my right hand high. "The winnah an' still cham-
peen!" he croaked.

My hand was tingling, and the knuckles hurt. I felt
them tenderly. I hadn't injured my hand, but I had hurt
it, and the knuckles ached for a few minutes. The
shark's nose had no more give than a block of wood.
That's exactly what it was like—as if I had taken a
good hard punch at a telephone pole. But I chased him
away.

We settled down for a while then. The sea was rough
and I was afraid the boat would tip over.

We hadn't eaten for a week now. Our last food was
the coconut we got on the twenty-first day, and what
strength we had left was ebbing faster. We began to
appreciate the luck we had had when we caught the
birds and fish. Those chances never came again.

Gene's eyes were the sharpest in the boat. In his afternoon watch, on this twenty-eighth day, he raised the
coconut alarm again. Instantly Tony and I had out the

paddles, and made our way cross-wind to where the big brown nut rose and dipped on the snapping blue waves. I shifted my shoe-paddle to the inboard hand and scooped the prize into the boat.

The fiber was softened by the water, as we had found with the other. We clawed the covering off with pliers and greedy hands. We drank, and wolfed the rich, white meat as fast as we could slice it loose. We divided the haul in equal shares, measuring with the knife. We scraped the inside clean, unwilling to waste the slightest speck.

When the meal was over we rehashed it in detail, commenting on the quality, the texture, and the taste. We tried to estimate its age, and argued over the distance it must have floated from the island where it grew. We speculated on the island itself, its probable position, and whether the Japs might have it. We thought we must be nearing land, and we made little bets on when we'd find another coconut, and who would see it first.

But that was our last food.

CHAPTER · TWENTY

TONY wanted to die on a calm day, but the weather was becoming increasingly worse. The winds were variable, and generally high. The sky was overcast much of the time. Squalls were numerous and nasty. This was the beginning of the hurricane we were to learn about later, the most disastrous hurricane remembered in the South Pacific. It was fortunate, perhaps, that we were unable to recognize the signs of what was in store.

When the clouds blackened and the wind rose, the sea grew angry and lashed us viciously. Even with the canvas anchor it was difficult to control the boat. We were continually drenched and often in danger of upsetting. Worst of all, we had little strength left for fighting. The weakness hit us all at once, and left our ravaged bodies full of pain. Our morale, too, was lowest when we needed it most.

The rain came often and mercilessly. The squalls were

cold now—miserably cold, and we huddled together to keep warm. We were almost without flesh, it seemed; when we lay down in the bottom of the boat for warmth we were wedged together, and our sharp bones bumped painfully. The only way I could stretch out was to lie in the middle of the boat, the two boys one on each side. Tony's hips would be punching into me on one side, Gene's knees and elbows digging me in the back. We could lie together in this position only a short while until our circulation would be cut off. Then we would have to get up and stretch to make our starved and sluggish blood move again.

Often we would deliberately leave several inches of water in the bottom of the boat, as it was warmer than the air. When we sat up, the swift wind blew needle-point spray that seemed to penetrate our tender skin. In our dry mouths, our foul-tasting teeth chattered until they ached.

None of us thought very much about talking and carrying on a conversation. We grew away from that toward the last. Things were becoming serious. We could see that our end was approaching, one way or another. We must be saved soon, or we would die.

Tony and I seemed to be able to take it a little better than Gene. He would beg us to talk to him, and then the only thing he was willing to talk about was food. I made a constant effort to be affable and agreeable with both boys, as I knew we were under a constant strain and I felt that it was up to me as leader to do all in my power to maintain good feeling and harmony amongst us, in an effort to ward off the tendency we were all showing, so obviously, to brood over our position. Clearly, our courage was beginning to fail us at this point.

When we had our sip of water in the middle of the day, we tried imagining it was coffee. The tiny drink would buoy our spirits, and we could conjure, in our minds, a good meal to go with it. Sometimes we would go to Gene's house and have a big dinner of his Missouri hickory-smoked ham with all the fixings. Another time we would visit Tony's, where we ate all kinds of Polish food. One of his favorite dishes was what he called "pigeon in a blanket," made by rolling hamburgers in cabbage leaves. It sounded good to us then, and we devoured it in our minds. Again, we would go to my ranch, Calavo, in La Mesa, and stuff ourselves with avocados and oranges.

Despite my own distaste for this self-torturing conversation, I didn't discourage it, for at least it occupied our minds more pleasantly than any other thoughts we had.

After the twenty-eighth day and the last coconut, we realized at last that we were starving. I am convinced that the small amount we ate contributed nothing toward maintaining our strength. The few unpalatable mouthfuls made our suffering worse, if anything, by stimulating the hunger and starting our juices to work against us.

Inevitably, we discussed cannibalism.

One of the boys suggested one day, "Suppose one of us starves to death—of course one of us would go first —what should we do with the body?"

Tony had shown a horror of being buried at sea on a rough day. The warsman knows, when he goes to sea, that he may not see land again. Many of us have seen a comrade's body given to the waves, and we are conscious that the same fate may await us any day. Tony had said that he wouldn't mind meeting Davy Jones on a calm, beautiful day—he'd be perfectly happy to go if the sun were shining and the sea was still.

Tony was the thinnest of us, and I think he had an idea that he would die first. Perhaps, also, he had a horror of being eaten. I think that may have been one of the reasons why he suggested now that we should jump over the side and end it all. When he recalled this later, he said he didn't think he really meant it— and again I believe him.

At any rate, we put the question before the house: If one of us should die, should the others eat his body?

One of the boys suggested that it might be a good idea to eat part of the dead man, anyway. We talked the proposition over at length. Finally we all agreed that the survivors should eat the heart, liver, and other such organs.

Today I don't believe that any of us had a real intention of stooping so. I'm sure I didn't, and I don't think the others did either. But it offered a new source of conversation to us, and we threshed it out thoroughly.

I kept my eyes closed most of the time, now, when the sun was out. Days and days of watching the glaring water had strained my eyes until now I could look into the distance for only a few seconds, then things would begin to blur. Afterward they pained me greatly, and finally I reached the point where even at night the reflection of the moon on the water hurt them.

In the fourth week I had noticed that my feet and legs were losing their sense of feeling. This began in the feet and moved upward, a little farther each day, until the partial paralysis reached my hips. Practically all of the time we spent sitting, or lying in the bottom of the boat, which required us to pull up our knees. Eventually I felt as if I had rheumatism. The suffering was intense when I tried to lie down in the tortuous position that the limited space required me to take.

The pounding of the choppy waves beneath the fabric bottom nearly drove me mad. Every night I thought: Tonight I am more tired than I have ever been before, so maybe this time I can sleep. And every night the monotonous, jarring hammer beneath me, coupled with the always unexpected drenching from above, drove me to sit up and wait for more favorable conditions. No more favorable conditions ever developed. As time went on, exhaustion closed around me like a tightening hand. I had to drive myself to think.

Fatigue, and pain of infinite variety, loosed the reins on my temper. When I spoke to one of the boys, and he didn't answer but continued staring straight ahead, I sometimes forgot that he was under the same strain as I, and I raged like a madman. These outbursts never lasted long; I had not the strength. There was never an answering violence in the boys; they had not the energy, or didn't care, or didn't know.

CHAPTER · TWENTY-ONE

ON the twenty-ninth day the old gray albatross returned and began introducing bad luck to us in large doses. At first I was glad to see him, a familiar thing. I wondered where he had been when the storm was at its height. He circled high above the boat, darting now and then to inspect a wave that rose to meet him.

The sea was rough and sullen. The wind had blown contrarily through the night, and I had left the sea anchor out, to hold us back and steady us. Right after sunrise I thought of the anchor first. It was the only means we had of controlling the boat, and after every misadventure I checked to see that it was safe. This morning I found that the drive of the high wind against the boat had pulled the jacket to the surface, where it lay collapsed. I started to pull it in, intending to shake it out and let it go again. Without its drag the small gale was sending us away from our direction, and I felt that every mile counted in our chance to live a little longer.

As I hauled in the anchor, a small fish came into view beneath the surface at the bow. It was the same kind as we had caught before.

Food!

I watched him warily. He swam under the boat.

As I got the anchor aboard, out he came again. He paused right in front of me. If I had had the knife I could have stabbed him. I turned to look for the knife. I fumbled in the tool pocket for several seconds, trying to keep an eye on the fish at the same time. He lay on the surface, resting.

I moved to the side of the boat, but in my weakness I was not quick enough. A flirt of his tail sent him drifting out of reach. I waited, and he held himself still, tantalizingly lifting and falling with the rolling waves. Finally he swung an inch or two closer and I lunged, but got nothing but water in the face for my pains. I lay across the gunwale for a moment, resting. I needed to gather myself to fix the anchor.

As I waited, a great spotted leopard shark, about seven feet long, poked his nose out of the water not six inches from my face. I drew back, startled. If I had had the nerve I could have snatched him by the gills. I hesitated for several seconds, and tried to make myself grab him, but I couldn't. The truth is, I was a little afraid of him. I was conscious of this, and a little disgusted, as he twisted and dived out of view beneath a gray-green wave.

I cursed my timidity. I probably couldn't have held the monster, but I might have hauled him into the boat before I was exhausted, and then he would have been a goner; we could have held him until he suffocated. That would have been a lot of meat, I reflected wearily. He weighed about a hundred pounds, I guessed.

The wind rose higher, and the waves came faster. The swells uncoiled like great green snakes and burst into white at the top, then fell apart with an angry roar. They rolled beneath the light raft and raised us up until we looked into a sickening depth. Then we would spin downward, sometimes missing the break, sometimes whirling in the wild white froth. We shipped water, gallons at a time, and bailed frantically with our hands. We watched the waves like surf-riders, rolling our weight from side to side as the combers tossed the boat like a toy. We learned to shift ourselves adroitly when the crest hit, to keep the raft in balance.

But the sea is cunning. It can bide its time, and spring like a beast. The wind was its ally.

The raft rose slowly as the comber uncoiled beneath us and a little to one side. The wind seemed to pause for breath. We eyed the wave's curling summit.

A wall of green laced with white, translucent as we saw it against the sky, collapsed all over us. Its weight made our ears ring, and filled our nostrils. Coughing and blinded, we fell across the gunwale. The wind, as if it had been waiting, blew a heavy gust that raised the raft and tipped it over.

We were in the sea again, a more fearsome sea than any of us had ever seen. We all had the same thought, I guess: to grab that raft. Once more we were fortunate. We clasped it in our arms, and held with all our strength. With the mad water pulling at my legs, I looked at the boys. Tony was holding on frantically. His eyes were closed, and he was saying a prayer in Polish. Gene's lips were stretched with his effort, and showed his teeth clenched.

"Hold on!" I screamed. I don't think I was heard in the howling wind and waves. It didn't matter.

I maneuvered around to the other side, holding my head down as waves dashed against my face. The sea was clubbing me, trying to beat me down. I pulled my head between my shoulders and took the stunning blows as groggy fighters do.

I got my hand beneath the boat and lifted. I felt as if my heart was stopping. I knew I had to do every little thing right, while in this maelstrom, or I'd die.

Again I tricked the wind. It swept beneath, filled the inside, and lifted the raft right side up, slamming its bottom against a slanted wall of sea.

We flung ourselves against the raft again. I somehow scrambled in, and grabbed Tony by both his wrists. I let myself fall to a sitting position, braced my feet, and pulled him in. Between us, then, we rescued Gene. All of us lay and panted, heads down.

Sometime later, maybe hours, I took the inventory. All our spare rags were gone, but the water-catching rags were there. Then—I missed the anchor.

This was a terrible blow. Now we could not control the raft except by rowing, and our last experience with rowing had so weakened us that I knew we would have to give it up except in the last extremity.

Our peril made my mind sharper. I went over our gear in search of anything that might make a suitable sea anchor, but the only likely thing I found was the piece of patching material, of the same fabric as the boat, about twelve inches long by six inches wide. I rigged it on the line, but I found at once that this makeshift would not do. For one thing, it would not sink deep enough; secondly, it was too small.

I tried putting the pliers on the line, also the few steel pieces remaining from the gun, in an arrangement like the tail of a kite. The weighted line held strongly, but it made our boat yaw back and forth in the trough of the sea, so that we shipped great quantities of water every time we hit a comber.

This was our last possibility, and I was determined to make it work. I left the new anchor out all day, but we had to bail constantly. By sundown I could see that we would not have strength to keep this up. Soon the water would begin to rise faster than we could sweep it out, and we would founder. Against my will, I did the only thing I could. There was a strong southwest wind blowing us directly opposite to our desires, but I took the anchor in and let the boat drift.

I thought: It's drift or drown.

We watched night fall, without joy. I noted, irrelevantly, that the albatross was feeding.

CHAPTER · TWENTY-TWO

WE passed a night of misery in the brewing hurricane. Without an anchor we were at the mercy of the wind, and it blew viciously. Many times we just missed tipping over again, by maneuvering our weight to shift the boat's center of gravity when the mountainous waves knocked us off balance. High combers kept breaking into the boat, half filling it every time. We scooped the water out with our twisted garments, although we thought we would freeze, naked in the cold, slashing rain.

Toward morning the gale slackened, but the sea still boiled. As dawn approached and I was able to see a few feet around, I marveled that we were still afloat among those giant wind-whipped swells. When full daylight came I saw that our world had closed around us. We were in the center of a small circle of agitated green water, under a dome of gray mist. We could not see far in any direction. Everywhere we looked the sea was in frenzied motion, countless white-topped peaks appearing, rolling, and bursting in a gush of foam.

When we stopped shipping water, we sat in the boat with our backs hunched against the rain and wind. We were still drifting to the northeast, making fast time away from where we wished to go.

We said very little to each other. We were hungry and disheartened.

Toward the middle of the morning we took the jacket, on which I had drawn our chart, and held it over our three heads to give a little protection from the chilling rain.

"Hold it careful, boys," I said. "If we lose this, we don't know where we are."

The canvas chart kept the rain off us a little bit, but our clothes were soaked and clammy, and plastered to our skin. I would have been glad to see the sun again, and wondered if I ever would.

"There's your albatross," Tony said.

I looked up, and saw the old gray bird sailing along above us, his wings spread wide, apparently oblivious to the rain and wind. I watched him for a while until my eyes began to hurt. I lowered my head, relaxing, and my beard scraped the sunburned triangle below my throat.

Something thumped me on the head. I sat still, and felt a heavy weight settling on the top of my skull. It moved slightly, and after a tense moment I realized what had happened.

The albatross had alighted on my head. He was pluming his bedraggled feathers there.

I sat very still, figuring what to do. The boys hadn't seen him yet. I considered whether to make a grab for him myself, or let one of the others try.

The chart's being over my head rather complicated matters. There was a chance that as I grabbed for the albatross my hand would become entangled in the canvas.

I studied the situation carefully, and decided to chance it.

Silently, I slid my right hand outward, gauged my aim as best I could since I was unable to see my quarry, and snatched quickly.

The albatross must have been squatting down as I reached for him, because my hand struck him in the breast. The blow knocked him backward into the water.

He floundered for an instant, righted himself indignantly, and rose above the water with a flap of his mighty wings. He flew away, high, then circled back as if to reconnoiter us.

"Jeez, you almost got him, though," Tony said.

I was feeling very glum, and bitter at my failure in this heaven-sent opportunity to obtain food that we all needed so badly. I was sorry I had not let one of the boys try to grab the bird. They could have seen him, whereas I could not.

"Well, I'm afraid he's gone," I said disconsolately.

"Cheer up, chief, it was a good try," Tony said.

"Wonder if we can't find a little more room in here?" Gene asked.

"Any change would help," Tony said. "I'm getting pretty stiff."

I myself was sore all over. We shifted our positions so that two of us sat with our backs against the forward thwart, while the third huddled among our knees.

"We'd be better off in a telephone booth," Tony said. "It'd be dry."

Gene and I mustered a feeble laugh at Tony's witticism. Then we sat silent a few moments as the rain beat on the chart we held over our heads, and the water ran down our necks in cold rivulets.

Tony spoke again.

"That damned albatross is getting familiar again," he said. "Look to starboard, chief."

I turned quietly, and there was our friend, sitting right alongside me in the water. He was feeding.

"Oh, God, one more chance," I said softly, not in supplication but in gratitude.

The huge bird drifted to within three feet of the boat, and ducked his head under the water. He held his beak and eyes submerged for all of ten seconds. It was as if he were inviting me to grab him.

I thought: If he keeps his head down that long, I'll wait until he does it again, and give myself more time.

I sat still until he came up for air. He looked about

him in the water, but didn't move his body. He seemed to find what he wanted, and jabbed his bill back into the water.

Without waiting longer than it took to gather my muscles for the effort, I dived over the side, my hands outstretched to grab the bird.

But I never finished the dive. My feet, instead of driving me forward, pushed the boat behind me. The next thing I knew, I was lying full length, face down. The whole front of me smarted from the smash against the water.

In my surprise and disappointment I couldn't think but I instinctively dropped my feet and spread my arms to keep myself afloat. My long body was being lifted by the choppy waves, and the boat was already several feet away. As I lunged for the raft I couldn't help looking for the albatross, who had escaped me for the second time in a way that was humiliating, and worse. The bird was fluttering away—taking his time about it, too— and I swear that if birds can laugh, the gray albatross was hooting at me.

Tony grabbed me by an arm, and I was quickly in the boat.

"Where's the chart?" I demanded immediately.

"It went over the side with you, chief."

I turned, but instantly I abandoned whatever idea I might have had of diving to retrieve the chart. In that sea, it was gone.

We were now without a single article of any use to us, except our anchor line, one water rag (badly tattered), a pair of pliers, and the pocketknife. We were without protection of any kind against the weather, except the sparse clothing on our backs.

I decided to strip off the useless oar pocket to make a covering for our heads. This I did. The piece of fabric thus obtained was almost square, twenty inches long by sixteen inches wide. It served us better than nothing.

It rained steadily all morning. Shortly after noon we hit a heavy squall, with high winds and a terrifying sea, and we tipped over again.

How we got back into the raft against the waves I don't know. When we did, we found that all our gear was gone—knife, pliers, our newly obtained head covering, the unsuccessful sea anchor, and our last rag. Now we had nothing to protect ourselves, nothing for bailing, nothing for catching food.

Our courage almost failed. This had been a day of horrible disaster.

Tony Pastula, bless his game soul, spoke up at last.

"Well, fellows," he said wryly, "it has all happened now, it looks like. What do you say we shake hands all around and start all over again?"

Gene and I instantly agreed. Crouching in the wobbling rubber tub, with the wind blowing icy rain at us in fire-hose gusts, we exchanged handshakes and declared to each other that this would be a new beginning.

CHAPTER · TWENTY-THREE

EVENING of the thirty-second day we got a shift of wind to the north. Night fell ominously. The sky was dark and threatening; the sea turned from gray to black. As we tumbled along uneasily, our way was lit by long, jagged streaks of lightning, each flash followed by a rolling thunder clap like cannon fire. The air was heavy and stirred sluggishly in the fitful breeze. The waves had lost their frenzy, but still rose high in powerful surges of slowly expanding force.

In the weird twilight, the sky was an awesome spectacle foreboding ill. I called it to the attention of the boys.

There were several layers of clouds, and each layer seemed to be traveling in a different direction. This was beyond the experience of any of us, and we could not imagine what it portended.

"Whatever it means," Tony said, speaking for us all, "it don't mean nothing good."

In my twenty-two years in the navy I had never seen a sky or sea like this, and I didn't like the look of things a bit.

"Better rest while we can," I advised the boys. "Any minute we'll have to bail."

We lay down in the bottom of the raft. The spray that broke on us was cold, and we squeezed ourselves together to keep the warmth of our bodies.

It rained often during the night. Each time we got up to bail and wring out our clothes again.

Tonight we talked more than usual, trying to cheer each other. We all realized, I think, that our spirits occasionally dropped near the danger point of lowness, and it became a game to see who could do the most to lift us out of our despondency. We made little jokes, forced and desperate.

We didn't mind the bailing. Our hips and shoulders were so numb and sore from lying wedged in the bottom of the raft that we actually welcomed the opportunity to get up and move our stiffened muscles. We suffered from lack of circulation. We had so little flesh that our veins were drawn across our bones. When we sat up, our blood would move, but this exposed us to the wind and spray. We chilled easily, so that after a moment we would be forced to lie down again in search of warmth.

Thus we passed the night. It seemed a long time until daylight came.

With morning, we saw that the sky was almost solidly overcast. We waited in vain for the sun to come out and warm us. Everything was gray, except our yellow raft. Its giddy color on the muttering, gloomy sea accentuated its incongruity.

The wind now had shifted to the northeast again, and was driving us along at a lively clip. This was more to our desire, but we couldn't be sure where we were, and couldn't have done anything about it if we had known. The only chart we had was in my head.

About eleven o'clock in the morning we hit a shower, heavy and as cold as ice water. The raft held water over our ankles when it ended.

We had lost the last of our rags in the last tip-over, so we took off all our clothes, mopped the bottom of the boat and wrung over the side, repeating until the raft was dry.

As we finished this tiresome chore the sun appeared, for the first time that day. In our chilled condition the rays felt good.

"Let's take a sun bath before we put our clothes on," I suggested.

The boys assented readily, and we lay against the sides to rest, for we were tired as well as cold. We stretched our clothes across the thwarts to dry.

After a while Tony spoke up nervously.

"Don't you think we'd better put on our clothes?"

I wasn't looking forward to it. They were damp.

"Well, it's pretty rough, you know," Tony argued. "The boat's liable to go over on us again."

The wind had risen and the waves were coming to a boil. The raft was bobbling like an orange rind.

I hesitated for a few seconds, and was just about to agree with Tony when a big comber caught us.

We were lifted high, the raft on such a slant that we had to grab the sides and thwarts to keep from falling out. As we started to slide down the long, sheer trough of the wave, the breaking crest gave us an extra push upward on one side. The wind caught beneath the rounded air chamber. There was a wild scramble of arms and legs, mad grasping, and a confusion of shouts.

"The clothes! The clothes!" I yelled frantically as I went through the air. The scornful wind snatched the words, and a great wave engulfed me.

My head was out of the water again, and somehow my hand was on the raft. Gene, it appeared, had never let go, and was hanging on desperately. Tony had fallen almost on us. I grabbed him by an arm.

The waves were flinging us about, pulling at our legs as if with hands. The raft was upside down.

Never letting go our handholds, we grouped ourselves together and at an unspoken signal heaved the raft upward, trying to keep our grasp on the upended gunwale at the same time. A comber thundered down and almost tore it from our grip.

Quickly, before the next wave came, we pushed upward again. The light raft went over this time, and I worked my way to the opposite side to hold it down while the boys climbed in.

For a few minutes we rested, panting, each with an arm locked across a thwart in case we tipped again. The blood was pounding in my temples. I couldn't breathe without pain.

My chest and torso ached, and, as I have explained before, I was perpetually half numb from the hips down. With a supreme effort of will I raised my head and rolled my body over so that I faced upward across the raft. The boys were lying still, heads down, twisted, inert, like dead men except for their loud and broken gasps for air.

I noted automatically that our weight was not all on one side, which seemed to be our greatest peril. The raft was riding evenly; although it pitched and swerved in continual jerky motion, the bottom was holding to the water. So I sank my head upon my breast and rested.

How long we lay this way I don't remember. I know that we were not in full possession of our minds. When I myself began to think again, it frightened me to realize how easily I slipped away.

I found myself as if awakened by a noise I half remembered from a dream. The boys were sitting up, revived but not disposed to talk. I tried to straighten on my haunches, and then the situation struck me like a blow.

All our clothes were lost—every thread and stitch, except, ridiculously, a police whistle that hung by a cord around my neck.

CHAPTER · TWENTY-FOUR

NOW on this day, our thirty-third in the raft, our position was desperate. Since we had lost even my last inadequate makeshift sea anchor, we had no means whatever of controlling our progress. From now on we would go where the wind sent us, and that might mean that we would float until the rubber boat finally rotted and burst. We had lost all our rags, so had no way of catching drinking water beyond what might lie in the bottom of the raft. We had nothing for bailing except our hands. We had one shoe-paddle left, two wallets which had somehow become wedged in the front of the raft, and my police whistle. I did not see how we could make any use of these.

The worst blow of all was the loss of all our clothes, and the piece of fabric we had been using to shade our heads. From now on we were entirely unprotected against the equatorial sun, and it was midsummer. We knew, too well, what the sun was going to do to us.

We thought we were in the vicinity of islands, but with no charts and no navigation instruments we could not be positive as to our position. As far as we could be sure, we might still be a thousand miles from land. Now we would never know where we were unless we actually sighted an island.

This was the one time during the entire trip that I was truly disheartened. In fact, I was just about ready to give up. I knew that the end of our voyage was very near; we must make an island in a day or two, or die.

Tony shared my gloom. He considered going over the side; it would be a quick death, without the torture that the sun had in store. But he changed his mind.

"We've come this far," he argued, "and by God we'll go on!"

Sitting glumly about the boat, discouraged, the three of us considered all the possibilities.

Loss of our clothes, our only shelter, seemed like a mighty hard blow for us to take at this stage of the game, after we had worked and schemed for so long to save ourselves.

The thought of what we had already gone through—that clinched the argument. We all agreed that neither this nor any other disaster which could overtake us now was sufficient reason for giving up the fight we had been making. Again we shook hands all around, and vowed we'd go on.

It was another night of chilling showers. We huddled together in the bottom of the raft, and talked a great deal to keep up our spirits, pursuing any subject that came into our minds.

After every shower we scooped out most of the water with our hands, and lay down again to keep warm. It took just about all our courage to stay cheerful. We knew that the end of our voyage was coming soon, one way or the other.

We were glad to see daylight in the morning. Although we knew we were going to be badly burned when the sun came overhead, we were anxious to warm ourselves. I tried to keep from thinking about what the sun was going to do to us later in the day. I preferred to let that worry come when it must.

The sun did not emerge from behind the clouds until about 8:30 o'clock in the morning. When it did, I stretched out on the forward thwart to warm myself and rest. Tony lay in the bottom, while Aldrich sat up, watching.

By this time, I thought, the navy must have given us up for dead. I learned later that this was true. I would have preferred another end, but this morning I let the sailor's fatalism have its play. I got to thinking over my past life. I had left home at the age of seventeen, worked my way around the country for a year at various jobs, then joined the navy. My older brother had been in the navy during the First World War, as they call it now.

I envied my older brother. I had been reared in a typical midwestern farm family, and the adventure of going to far places in uniform appealed to me. I tried several times to enlist, but first I was too young, then too thin, to make the grade. As I grew I put on weight, and finally got in at nineteen. I had no idea then of making the navy my career; I just wanted to serve a "hitch" for the experience.

That was twenty-two years ago. The navy had been good to me, and I was glad to die in the service, the warsman's way, if die I must.

I scooped up a bit of the indigo sea in my palm, and drank it. Toward the end I could stand a bit of sea water; my system seemed to be in need of salt. I blamed the sun for this.

I had shed two sets of skin prior to the time we lost our clothes. I was in the process of building a new set now, and the tender underskin was still exposed. Lying there entirely unprotected, I began to smart all over my body. My loins and midriff, which had never been sunburned before in all my life, turned scarlet in a half hour. Before the day was over this part of me looked as if it had been seared with a red-hot iron. The rest of my body, which had been protected somewhat by my rotting clothes, burned almost as severely.

The boys were in the same state. The scalding torture we had felt on our faces, hands, and arms now covered our bodies, every inch. The clouds had rolled away and the sea threw back the glare, so that everywhere we turned there was solid heat. I shifted my position frequently to take all advantage I could of the shade of my own body, and to try to keep from exposing the same area too long, but this did little good. The sun hit us practically all over, all of the time. I felt as if I were on fire. My body will always bear the scars of that cooking.

"Good Lord!" Gene said. "Look at that shark!"

I shaded my aching eyes against the sun, and saw a great black dorsal fin cutting the water a few yards from the boat. It was the largest shark I had ever seen.

He came close to the surface, and I whistled soundlessly when I made out the size of that sinuous, powerful body. I estimate that he was not less than fifteen feet long, and must have weighed upward of a thousand pounds.

"If he hits the boat, it's good-by," Gene said.

"Don't attract his attention," I whispered.

He cruised about the boat for about twenty minutes, then went away.

The sun began to hit Tony.

He was lying in the bottom of the raft, the back of his hand lying across his eyes. Suddenly he took his hand

[173]

away, and sat up, listening. He seemed to be looking far
off. He smiled slightly.

"Hey, chief," he said softly. "I hear music."

Humor him, and maybe he'll snap out of it, I thought.

"What kind of music, Tony?" I asked casually.

"Beautiful—like a choir of angels!"

He slid back into the bottom of the raft and closed
his eyes again, still smiling.

CHAPTER · TWENTY-FIVE

ALTHOUGH we had divided our days into two-hour watches, I was up and vigilant myself most of the time until my eyes began to fail. Now, because of that and my general physical condition, I was forced to let the man on watch take full responsibility for the boat while I conserved my dwindling energy for my own two-hour shift. Thus I lay on the forward thwart this thirty-fourth morning, turning uneasily under the sun so that my body would burn evenly and I would not suffer unnecessarily from overexposure of any one area more than another. Gene was on watch; Tony was lying in the bottom trying to shade his face —his delirium when he heard the music seemed to have passed.

It was about ten o'clock. The sky was hot and clear as a blue flame. The wind was steady, and the boat was rising and falling slowly on long, gentle swells. The sun was just now approaching the fullness of its anger.

We topped a wave, and in that brief instant while we seemed to hang suspended before the long downward slide began, Gene spoke for the first time since taking the watch.

"Chief," he said, "I see a beautiful field of corn."

I didn't even look up. I thought sadly that the boy's mind had finally gone, and I wished he had taken my advice to cover his head when we first went into the raft.

Without moving, I cast my eyes about the sea, but we were in the trough and I saw only the rumpled carpet of waves. It was possible, I said to myself, that Gene was seeing a mirage: the sun does play tricks on you sometimes. At any rate I was not surprised that Gene was affected. There was nothing I could do for him, so I paid no more attention.

After a few minutes, when we had risen to the next crest, he spoke again insistently: "Sure enough, chief!— I see something green in the distance!"

With this statement, so rationally put in his Missouri drawl, it dawned upon me suddenly that perhaps he did see something. I looked hard, but could still see nothing in the tumbling sea. Tony was looking too, but had not spoken. I tried to stand up, and found I couldn't balance on my cramped and crooked legs. I asked the boys to hold me upright.

We stood, the three of us, in the center of the boat, the boys each with one hand against the side and an arm around my waist, holding me erect with their shoulders while I steadied myself with arms around their necks.

We came to the summit of the next large swell. Sure enough, in the distance I could see something green. As Gene had said, it was beautiful. I instantly recognized it as an island, one of the low, verdant atolls of the far South Sea. I let out a hoarse whoop and turned to Gene, tightening my arm about his neck.

"Boy," I said exultantly, "you have won yourself a dinner!"

Tony took a deep breath, and let it go out noisily, trying to repress his joy.

"Well," he said, "thank God—and it's about time."

We were still far off. The island appeared as a low shelf of green—coconut trees, I guessed, and I was right. Chartless, we had no idea what the island was, whether it was inhabited, or whether it was in friend or enemy's hands.

The wind had risen strongly, making long and prominent streaks on the water, which gave me an excellent gauge of the exact wind direction. I took a bearing on the island, compared it with the wind direction, and found that our course of drift was carrying us about ten degrees to the right of the island.

We realized, of course, that this was our God-given chance for refuge, so, weak as we were, we saw nothing for it but to row. I took the port side of the raft, using our one remaining shoe-paddle. Gene and Tony paddled together on the starboard side, using their hands only.

We turned to with a will, rowing across the wind to make up for the distance by which the wind would cause us to miss the island if we simply drifted. In this manner we were able to make about one knot across the wind while we were being driven about five knots downwind.

It was fortunate indeed that we were able to see the island from such a distance. If we had been much closer when we began to row, the wind would have taken us past it because we would not have been able, by our feeble paddling, to compensate sufficiently for the drift.

We rowed all day, exactly across wind at 90 degrees to our sailing direction. I kept watching the island at intervals. We found it better to row facing the stern of the raft, pushing the water behind the boat with a forward sweep of our arms, so I had to stop rowing occasionally and turn to keep my bearing.

At first we thought there was only one island, but as we approached we saw that there were two, with a wide gap of water between. It was easy to make a choice. We took the nearer island.

By one o'clock our progress was visible. The waves were longer and crested in knifelike ridges that curled and broke in a thunderous gush of white foam. There was danger of our tipping over any time one of these breakers got behind us, but, while they were in front, the spray blowing backward enabled me to judge the wind exactly.

Suddenly Tony let out a screech. His hand flew out of the water and over his head as if jerked by a string. He half turned, holding the hand tenderly.

"Chief, a shark hit my hand," he yelled, his voice shaking slightly.

Gene and I hardly hesitated in our rowing.

"Did it bite you?" I asked.

"No," he said, looking and testing his fingers.

"Then to hell with it," I said. "Let's go on rowing!"

Without another second's hesitation he jabbed his hand back into the water, deep, and we went on rowing.

As we came up on the island, I thought it couldn't possibly be anything but a desert atoll, although it was a lovely green and apparently stuck up pretty well out of the water. When we came within six or eight miles I saw what I thought was a ledge of rocks above the white beach. I figured then that it must be a volcanic island, and we might find shelter in a cavern. This would also mean that the island was marked on the map, and might be visited—by our own or friendly forces, I hoped. There was still the uncertainty that this might be in the Japanese mandate, and if that was so I could see our doom. However, as long as we were determined to get there, I preferred to think that it was uninhabited.

The closer we approached, the better the island looked to me. I could see two or three especially tall trees that towered above the others. We wondered if they might be coconut trees, but that seemed too much to hope. Until I was close enough to identify them honestly as palms, I didn't dare believe they were.

I was sure, at any rate, that there would be lots of birds on the island, which meant eggs and possibly young birds that we could capture. I thought too that there might be mussels, and possibly fish in abundance that we would rig spears to catch.

Aldrich's eyes were still in good condition. As we came in closer, perhaps within three miles of the curving beach, he turned and took a long look. We had seen by this time that the island was not so high as we had thought at first.

"Chief," Gene said, "those aren't rocks on the beach. They're shacks."

I looked again, and again I decided they were rocks.

"Wishful thinking, Gene," I said. "If they were shacks it would mean that the island is inhabited. They still look like rocks to me."

Tony had his revenge.

"Hell with the rocks," he said. "Row!"

The waves were very high, and we could see the island only when we came to a crest; when we dipped to the valley of the waves, the island sank from sight. The buoyant raft rode the roughening sea so easily that it appeared as if the island and not we were rising and falling steeply in an even rhythm, while the raft lay perfectly still.

When we were about a mile from the island I saw from the wind streaks and blowing foam that we were directly upwind, and that the stiff breeze would land us at the center of the beach without assistance.

"Okay, boys," I said. "We can knock off the rowing."

We stopped and turned about, to watch our progress. We were completely exhausted, I know now. We had been rowing all day on will power alone, but we were so intent on reaching this island that we didn't realize our terrible weakness, and rose above it.

"Well," Gene said joyfully, "are they shacks or rocks?"

He was right. They were shacks.

From now on it was just a matter of drifting in the wind. I kept a close eye on the bearings by the wind streaks, to be sure that we hit the beach.

We became conscious of a steady, sullen thunder that seemed to grow in volume. I realized after a moment that it was surf breaking over a barrier reef, and I feared we were in for a little trouble. As we drifted closer I was able to see, and immediately gave the order to square away for a possible tip-over.

I had seen natives bring outrigger canoes over heavy surf in Hawaii, but those breakers were not nearly so murderous as these appeared. The nearer we approached the reef, the larger the breakers looked. I soon saw that our eyes were not deceiving us. These waves were building up characteristically in rows one behind the other, each coming to its turn as leader of the irresistible flow to shore.

The leading wave gained swiftly in height and speed as the wall of coral dammed the powerful tide that pushed against it, and the rushing tons of water found their only outlet upward. When the wave reached the reef it was about thirty feet high. The crest began to curl dangerously, seemed to hesitate the merest fraction of a second, then fell forward over the natural dam. There was a roar like a cannon shot as the mass of water smashed, and a great burst of foam spewed forward in a straight line of boiling white which diminished in size but held its form until it washed high on the beach, far ahead.

These rows of waves were building behind us now. Our only hope was to paddle over the reef ahead of the breaker—that is, in the interval between two waves.

We were fortunate enough to pass over the reef at the one brief instant when the surf was not breaking. We could have been dashed against the rocky bottom, or the ledge itself, if we had been caught in that wild churning of forces when the breaker crashes from its great height. As it was, we did not come out unscathed.

The breaker caught the raft behind. The heavy blow

of the rushing foam against the stern sped us up the sloping rear of the smaller, shoreward-speeding wave ahead. Instead of sliding down its front, we shot straight out into the air.

The raft turned a complete flip-flop. When we saw it next it was speeding landward like a chip before the surf. The three of us were in the water.

I can remember spinning head over heels three or four times, and raking along the floor of the sea. Whether it was sand or rock I don't know, but afterward I discovered that a patch of skin about six inches in diameter had been scraped from the center of my back. Gene and Tony, I learned, were going through exactly the same thing. Tony said this was the first time he had ever had his eyes open underwater.

"Everything was green and pretty," he said.

After a threshing by the water that left me only half conscious, I found myself sitting on a flat ledge of coral rock. The raft, I saw, was upside down again and was heading for the beach about a hundred yards away from me. Gene and I were close together, and we still had about three hundred yards to go to reach solid ground. Tony was about fifty yards behind us.

None of us was able to stand. I tried to raise myself on my feet, but couldn't get my balance. Then I found that the current was skidding me along on my bottom. Gene, even with me and to my right, also let himself drift and we kept abreast.

I heard a call for help, and looked back. It was Tony. Being unable to swim, he thought he was going to drown. When I waved and yelled, he realized he was out of danger, and thenceforth scooted along like Gene and me. I imagine things had happened so fast that when Tony got into shallow water he didn't realize it, and possibly he was hollering as a nervous reaction from the terrific beating his shrunken body had taken in the surf.

We caught the boat at the very edge of the beach, and grabbed the anchor line. Crawling on all fours, we dragged ourselves from the last persistent clutch of the sea, and somehow hauled the raft behind us.

We tried to stand upon our feet, but couldn't. We were terribly dizzy from exhaustion; the whole world seemed to be spinning around us. We lay on the beach together, faintly conscious of the broken coral that was cutting our flaming, sunburned flesh as our bodies jerked in the effort to breathe.

When I was able to look about, the sun was low.

A short distance away several rotting piles had been driven into the sand, evidently placed there by someone for tying up boats. The three of us took hold of the anchor line, dragging the raft with one hand while with the other we pulled ourselves painfully, inch by inch, over the jagged coral to the row of wooden stakes. I felt each of these ancient poles, selecting the one that was most solid. We tied the boat to that.

There were several thatched huts a few yards from where we lay.

Grasping one of the pilings with both hands, I pulled myself to my knees.

"Boys," I said, "you know there may be Japs here waiting for us."

They raised their heads and nodded.

I looked at each one closely. They were gazing steadily into my eyes. Tony gestured toward the police whistle, still on a cord about my neck.

"If we have to scatter," he suggested calmly, "two blasts on the whistle will be the signal to meet wherever you are."

It was agreed.

We were too weak to try to find food, so we decided to rest for the night in one of the shacks.

I chose three long pieces of driftwood lying about that were best suited to my purpose, and handed one to each.

"If there are Japs on this island," I said, "they'll not see an American sailor crawl. We'll stand, and march, and make them shoot us down, like men-o'-warsmen."

Using the sticks of driftwood as canes to support us, we got on our feet. Three abreast then, myself in the middle, we walked to the nearest hut and went in.

EPILOGUE · THE ISLAND

THE shack had a good roof over it, made of woven fibrous material, apparently coconut, and covered six or eight inches deep by layers of coconut leaves laid with the stems up in a sort of shingle arrangement. The framework was formed of upright poles tied together by a fiber that we assumed to be either coconut or some other native growth. The building was about eight feet wide by ten feet long. Some two and a half feet off the ground were three poles that ran the width of the shack. There was nothing under them. There were two smaller poles connecting the uprights, not nailed but lashed with some sort of native-made string. The shack had a ridgepole and arch beams, as any other house would have. The walls were of matting. Just overhead were rafters, and resting on them were three roughly hewn planks about twelve feet long by eight feet wide. On the floor we found a pile of coconut mats three feet wide by eight feet long.

We didn't inspect the shack closely that night; we were too weak to pay much attention to our surroundings. Our main trouble, physically, was in trying to balance ourselves, but by holding onto the uprights we managed to get about. However, I had enough strength left to get those three planks down from the rafters, to form the framework for a makeshift bed of mats.

We piled about half the mats on the planks, and Tony and I slept there that night. With the rest of the mats we made a bed on the ground for Gene.

Right outside our shelter there was a dense grove of coconut trees, and Gene decided to gather some nuts. When he got outside the wind was so strong that he couldn't stand against it, even by using his stick to lean on, and the coral hurt his feet, so he had to give up and come back to the shack. It was with reluctance that we gave up the idea of food that night, but we thought the wind would die down by morning.

I spied a couple of chickens in the jungle, but of course they frightened easily, and we were in no condition to attempt chasing them down.

About a half hour later Gene saw two men approaching up the beach, perhaps three hundred yards away. He thought they saw us, but they turned and went in the other direction.

By now the rising wind was blowing gusts of rain into

our shelter, so we rigged one of the coconut mats to protect us. We didn't know it at the time, but this heavy wind from offshore was to develop into a hurricane the next day.

The wind rose gradually, and it rained steadily. We spent a miserable night. The wind kept blowing the mats with which we tried to cover ourselves, and the rough, woven fiber scratched painfully against our sunburn. We were unable to sleep at all.

The next morning early, the first thing I did was to look around the shack and try to patch it where the wind, during the night, had blown off the siding. In casting about for materials for this repair, we found several fishlines in the rafters, with poles, but I refused to use them. I knew how the natives would feel about our breaking their lines, which were probably not easy to obtain in these parts. Instead, we gathered up some coconut leaves. Using the fiber from these, we patched the mat walls pretty well. The shack was well made, but seemed to be very old. It was rotting in places. I thought it must have stood there a long while. While looking about in the rafters I found a thick book in a strange language. It developed that this was a native Bible.

While we were still working on the patching job, we saw a native coming toward us from the beach. It had stopped raining. I grabbed my police whistle, which I had laid on the ground the night before, and blew a loud blast. The native stopped and looked at us, evidently aghast. It was obvious that he couldn't understand our being there.

After I blew my whistle two or three more times, he finally gathered his wits and ran up to see what was going on. We were sitting on the floor, leaning against the wall where we had been patching the mats. The native stared, fascinated. We all pointed to our mouths, trying to signify that we were hungry. He could see from our emaciated condition that we were in a bad state, so it didn't take him long to get the idea. He held up his hand reassuringly, and dashed off into the coconut jungle.

In a few minutes he was back, with several coconut kernels. I have never seen this particular cultivation of coconut anywhere but on this island. As I learned later, the baby coconut tree sprouts from a nut. When it has grown to a height of perhaps two and a half feet, the little plant is broken off. Then the natives crack open the nut, and it is filled entirely with a white, fibrous, vegetablelike substance. The coconut meat as we know it has entirely disappeared and has been replaced by this new growth, which is very easy to digest.

The native broke open the kernels and handed them to us. We snatched them and began munching immediately. I have never tasted anything more appetizing than those coconut kernels were that morning.

As we ate, the native made signs to us that he was going for help. He pointed to my police whistle, and held out his hand, smiling encouragingly. I gave him the whistle, and immediately he turned and ran off among the coconut trees, tooting the whistle vigorously. We looked at each other in great relief. At least the natives were friendly.

Our visitor was gone for perhaps a half hour. He returned with a party of several natives and a man who seemed to be the leader. This was the resident commissioner. Not knowing who we were, he had brought assistance in case we might turn out to be enemies.

I should explain here, perhaps, that as this account is written the events are still so recent that the navy intelligence considers it wiser for the security of our country that I withhold the identification of the island on which we landed, and the close location of the particular area of the South Pacific in which our adventure occurred. I can say, however, that the island was a tiny one, and so far from the trade routes or any other regular contact with the world that probably few who read this chronicle have ever heard of it.

At any rate: The first native recognized from our eyes that we were white men; by our burned skins he could not tell whether we were white, brown, yellow, red or black. He was quite sure, however, that we were not Japanese. He told the commissioner that he thought we were New Zealanders or Australians, so of course the commissioner expected us to be from allies of his country, as of course we were. He was taking no chances, though, and brought some man power along. There are no weapons on the island except knives.

The commissioner's first question was as to our nationality. Upon learning that we were American sailors, he showed his delight immediately. He explained, then, several peculiar aspects of our experience with the shack. In the first place, we had got into the only "tabu shack" on that section of the island. The various sheds we saw were for the storing of copra—in fact, there were about four tons of copra in the shacks at this time—but the one we had staggered into was the only shack that had a tabu: it was reserved for the higher ranking men of the island people. The natives were not only afraid to enter, they hesitated even to come near. The two natives of the night before, who Gene thought had seen us, did see us indeed, but they were afraid to say so for fear they would incur the wrath of their chief for venturing so near the forbidden.

The commissioner was curious as to how we had reached this particular part of the island. Had we walked there? We merely turned and pointed seaward. He was astounded. That, he said, was impossible! He could not believe we had come upon this beach from the sea. No one had ever come over that reef and lived to tell the tale!

It was our turn to be astonished. But after a surprised glance at each other, we pointed to our little raft, tied to the piling near the shack.

[191]

The commissioner walked out excitedly and took a look at the raft. He examined it carefully, feeling it all over with his hands, the natives chattering among themselves and looking back at us wonderingly. Then he came slowly back into the shack, put his hands on his hips and grinned down at us—he just grinned, speechless, shaking his head from side to side. We were now beginning to feel like curiosities for fair.

The commissioner explained that it was considered impossible for any man to come over that reef. There was a lookout tower on this beach, he said, and it was constantly manned by sharp-eyed natives on the watch for enemy craft, but as a rule they didn't consider it necessary to pay any attention to the impassable reef. For this reason, and also, perhaps, because our boat was so small, our fight against the waves and our last faltering march across the beach had gone unnoticed by the practiced watchers only a few yards off.

Our dialogue meant nothing to the natives, who spoke no English, but they knew that something unusual was afoot. When the commissioner explained to them who we were and what we had done, when they were told that we had actually come in over this reef in such a craft, they just stood around with their mouths open, staring at us as if we were supermen, or gods.

I was becoming a little embarrassed by their awe-stricken regard, so I tried to explain to the commissioner that our flat-bottomed, air-borne raft drew no water, and thus enabled us to cross the giant breakers where the heavy, native-built canoes might fail. The commissioner just shook his head again, his admiring grin spreading until I thought it would cut his face in two. The natives were still staring at us, saying nothing but "Oh" and "Ah."

At length the commissioner gave an order in the island language, and the husky, handsome brown natives gathered us into their arms like babies and set off with us at a swift pace.

We went toward the leeward side of the island, passing through beautiful groves of coconut trees and other tropical growth. I still was able to take some interest in what I saw as we went along, and I noted numerous taro beds.

The natives carried us a mile or more until we arrived at the commissioner's residence on the leeward side. The house stood on the highest point on the island, about forty feet above sea level. I learned that we were on one of the tiny atolls that dot the South Seas. The particular group to which this one belonged is one of the most isolated in all the South Pacific. There is more than one island in the group, but the others are deserted, and are visited only for the gathering of coconuts for the copra trade. Yesterday, in choosing one of the two visible islands as our objective, we had the fortune to pick the only inhabited one within many hundreds of miles.

We learned, when we were able to check our reckonings later, that we had completely circled the entire small group of islets before sighting our first land on the thirty-fourth day. In all, we covered approximately one thousand miles in the raft, but actually, from the point at which we landed our plane to this island the distance was about 750 miles.

We received a warm welcome from the commissioner's wife. She put us to bed at once in a large room at one end of the beautiful wide tropical-style building, and set about preparing us our first real meal since we left the ship.

This was the kind of house they try to duplicate in the South Seas movies. It was built of native hardwoods, so hard, the commissioner told us when we were able to talk more, that the termites wouldn't attempt to bite into it, taking any other kind of wood in preference. The framework was constructed of upright poles, all uniform in size, four to five inches in diameter. The poles were smooth and round and didn't seem to taper, so evidently this wood comes from a straight, high tree. No nails were used in the construction: everything was tied together with some kind of cord that resembled rattan. The sides and ceilings were made of beautiful hand-woven coconut panels. The roof over this intricate matwork consisted of layers of coconut leaves piled six or eight inches deep, like the roof of the shack we had

found. It was proved to us later that this roof was wind-
and rainproof.

The roof extended out and down from the sides of
the house to a distance of perhaps ten feet, giving about
seven feet clearance between the ground and the edges
of the eaves. There were windows in the places where
one would expect windows to be, but these had no
panels, screens, or glass, just frames through which the
trade winds wafted the delightful fragrance of tropical
flowers.

There were lots of mosquitoes, of course, but over
our three beds there was a huge net that kept out the
buzzing pests. Each evening servants would come in
and lower the nets for us, then with fanlike brushes
would drive out all the mosquitoes that had collected in
the room.

The meals were prepared in two huts in the yard, one
for cooking and the other for baking. Our gracious
hostess had her kitchens going like beehives a few minutes after our arrival.

The commissioner's wife had just enough coffee left
in her supply to make us one pot, which she gave us
immediately. When I tasted my first sip of coffee I was
able to believe, at last, that it was all true and not one
of those nightmares I used to have when I dozed in the
raft. We were really safe—it seemed impossible to believe, but that welcome cup of coffee was the convincer.

Lying there in civilized beds, we realized for the first

time what an ordeal we had come through, as evidenced by the physical conditions and reactions which now pressed themselves upon our consciousness. Our skinned backs and cooked hips kept us in constant torment for many days, and we found ourselves still unable to sleep at first.

Now that we were relieved of the spiritual compulsion, the overpowering drive from inward, that makes a man fight for his life against any odds, the ills and ravages of the body asserted themselves at once with a violence that stripped our nerves and left us helpless. We were dizzy for several days, and when we dropped to sleep briefly we had nightmares that surpassed in horror even those we had experienced in the raft.

Our legs had been so long doubled up in the raft, with little room to stand and none to walk, that as we abandoned our tired bodies to complete relaxation now they froze into the sitting position. We were able to straighten them after a week, but until then I lay most of the time on my back with my knees in the air, as I had seen my friend lie in sick bay aboard the ship, the day I had the presentiment that I would sometime be in the same position. That strange warning from somewhere—it had come true on this island.

I knew, though, that we were not to die. As for the boys, I had to warn them not to overdo the eating. We were going to be all right.

The commissioner was gone a great deal that day. We

soon learned that he was very much concerned over the fact that the barometer was dropping rapidly while the wind seemed to be increasing. The tall, slim palms were threshing back and forth like whips. The roar almost drowned the excited voices of the natives, who were running about securing their possessions, for it was plain that this was to be a disastrous storm.

By evening the gale had built to a hurricane. The surf was crashing like a series of small tidal waves against the tiny coral island. The thunderous boom of the sea, and the wind howling through thousands of palm trees, combined in an overpowering din that dominated all else and seemed to make the whole island shake. Then the rain was hurled against our house like tremendous buckets of marbles.

The commissioner's house was substantial and stood the ruthless beating without injury, but the natives' little homes were lifted from the ground and tumbled about like toys. Many of them ended as mere heaps of sticks and straw tangled among hundreds of fallen coconut palms.

There were about seven hundred natives on the island, and from what I observed now and later I believe every man, woman, and child of them was badly frightened that night. The commissioner instructed the native chief to move his people from the low part of the island, where the principal village was located, to the higher ground around the government house. They came, bringing as much of their possessions as they could carry in the storm. The commissioner's residence stood in a big grove of coconut palms, and we were worried that one of them might fall upon the house and cave it in. There were hundreds of natives taking refuge in the grove, and why none was struck by a falling tree I'll never understand; outside of superficial cuts and bruises, suffered as the wind flung them about, they all came out of it unhurt although many lost all their possessions and some became ill from exposure.

The trees fell like jackstraws. Many of those that did not blow over were stripped of their fronds, leaving them grotesquely high waving stumps. All the nuts that were on the trees dropped, of course, whether they were ripe or not.

In the rain, all the commissioner's fuel supply for cooking was soon wetted. As a result, our distressed hostess was unable to give us a great deal to eat except coconuts during the hurricane. She did manage to keep tea brewed, and once we ate dumplings which she steamed in her oven as the only available substitute for bread. The next morning she managed to get us two eggs each. Those were the last; the hurricane stopped the hens from laying. The second morning she made a pudding of arrowroot, one of the island staples. Of course we had lots of taro, which these islanders cook like potatoes—they do not make poi from taro as the Hawaiians do. She fixed coconut in various appetizing ways, but hungry as I was I found her coconut "cream" too rich for my taste and could drink little of it. I did consume enormous quantities of the coconut milk.

Taro appeared to be the island's staff of life. The commissioner had his own taro beds on high ground, but they were small and were expected to supply only the needs of the household. The natives did their cultivating on the lower lands, where they might be washed out if the wind rose high enough to blow the sea over the island. That is exactly what happened. On the second day of the storm the great waves rushed inland, completely destroying all the taro. This disaster alone would have left the islanders in a serious plight.

The hurricane lasted three days, and the damage that it did in that time was enormous. On the fourth morning, when the tumult of wind and rain had left the battered and bedraggled little island behind, the commissioner made a tour of inspection and came back with a grave face.

He estimated that a third of the coconut trees on the island had been blown down. Those left standing were so badly punished that it would be two years, he estimated, before they would be in condition to bear again. All the island's taro was killed except his own home garden, and all the banana trees were destroyed beyond repair.

The commissioner explained, very worried, that the island was low on provisions of all sorts, because there had not been a supply ship along in some time, owing to the war. There was a little rice, flour, tea, sugar and salt, but the stock of canned goods was almost gone. His wife had used the last tins of carrots and peas to make a stew for us our first day on the island. Chickens were still plentiful, and there were wild pigs, but of general provisions the islanders now had a supply sufficient for only two weeks.

Nevertheless, the natives, a brave and generous people, began pouring gifts of food upon us as soon as the hurricane had subsided. They remained carefree and confident even in the face of the impending famine. The native who had found us was typical. With his home gone, his gardens ruined, and no boat coming until no one knew when, he sat down and wove for me a beautiful coconut hat, with a band of beaded shells. He gathered somewhere a basket of coconuts, another basket of taro, and two chickens, one live and one cooked, and presented them to us.

When the other natives heard of this, they all dropped their cares and began streaming up to the commissioner's house with all sorts of gifts. Among them were several intricate shellwork hatbands and other trinkets, coconut mats, and other articles of native handicraft, at which they are unequaled.

The commissioner, not to be outdone, made each of us a present of genuine South Sea pearls.

Many of the natives brought gifts of food, usually a

chicken either alive or cooked, and in some cases both. These chickens looked like Plymouth Rocks, except that their legs were considerably longer. They are apparently good layers, and their meat leaves no complaint.

One native brought us a quarter of a pig freshly killed. This pork tasted different from any I had ever eaten before. It tasted more like chicken. The fat didn't contain much grease, and the lean meat was very tender. I learned that the island swine, after weaning, are allowed to run loose in the jungle, where I presume they live mostly on coconuts. The newborn pigs are allowed to suckle the sow only seven days; then they are taken away and are fed the same preparation of coconut milk that the native mothers give their babies. This is not the clear liquid from the inside of the mature coconut, which is what we call the milk; the islanders prefer the liquid obtained by taking a spoon and working on the juicy meat of the coconut kernel I have already described.

These natives are curious, friendly, and entirely unspoiled by contact with the ways of civilization. They have no firearms, but have big knives which the men handle with extreme skill. The men all smoke cigarettes, which they make by cutting up plug tobacco and rolling it into a slip of dried pandanus leaf. We were hungry for a smoke, of course, and soon learned the art. Smoking is their only civilized vice. They have no liquors.

After the first three days, when we were able to sit

on the veranda for our meals, the islanders gathered in great swarms to watch us eat. When they could get near us, they would stand about for hours looking at us, without a word. This was embarrassing to us at first, but we soon got used to them and paid no attention. One woman I remember particularly. She watched us for three days without a letup, just leaning on her elbows and gazing.

Under the kind and skillful care of the commissioner's wife we recuperated amazingly. Strength began to flow back into our muscles, and in a few days we were able to straighten our legs, then to walk with only a barely perceptible unsteadiness. We were still weak, of course, and were to remain so for some time, but mentally we seemed quite normal, all of us, and that relieved a worry I had had.

I could feel the weight growing back on my bones, and I could see Gene and Tony putting on pounds by the day. In fact, the most serious difficulty any of us had then was to keep from gorging on the food that the natives were continually putting before us.

When it no longer tired me too much to talk, I had long conversations with the commissioner about the island, and the serious food shortage he and his people faced because of the hurricane. With war conditions as they were in the Southwest Pacific, he didn't know when he could expect relief. I was becoming a bit anxious, too, about getting back home to the Pacific Fleet where I belonged. The commissioner then said that he had radioed an urgent plea for help, but had no answering word that he could take as assurance of immediate help.

Radioed? What! I had been almost a week on the island and didn't know there was a radio!

I went into action without delay. It seemed that the government had installed a small radio transmitter on the island, and had sent a trained native of one of the larger islands in that area to man it for the duration of the war.

Straightway I met this operator. He had some real cigarette tobacco and we discussed matters over my first honest-to-goodness civilized smoke. The languid South Sea air got a message to carry in a hurry. I made my report to my commanding officer, and went back to rest and recuperate, confident that we'd get some action now. We did.

Seven days from the date of our arrival on the island, there was an American warship offshore, and pretty soon we were shaking hands with the commander.

The ship that rescued us also saved the island. The vessel left a badly needed supply of food, and the natives' troubles were over. The commissioner's gratitude was unbounded. We were warm friends by now. When we

shook hands and said good-by, I resolved that someday I would go back to that lovely, generous place,
and if God is willing I will.

The rest of the story is mainly one of interviews,
some with the press and many with doctors, who seemed
surprised to find nothing much wrong with us.

Oh, yes—on the way home we were attacked by a
Jap submarine. We drove her off.

Dixon received the Navy Cross for "extraordinary heroism, exceptional determination, resourcefulness, skilled seamanship, excellent judgment and highest quality of leadership." Pastula and Aldrich were cited for "extraordinary courage, fortitude, strength of character and exceptional endurance."

—THE NEW YORK TIMES

AFTERWORD

After Dixon, Aldrich, and Pastula bade farewell to Commissioner Geoffrey Henry and his Polynesian wife, who with their native charges had given unstintingly of their meager resources to feed them, the USS *Swan* (AVP 7) took the three survivors to a hospital at American Samoa for recovery from malnutrition and severe sunburn. On arrival, an Army general told them that they could have anything they wanted—money, clothes, special food, anything was theirs for the asking. One man asked only for "something to put my gear in."

"In actuality," said the general, "a Bull Durham sack would have been sufficient to hold everything they owned."

They then returned to Hawaii, where a debriefing was held. All three had been recommended for the Navy Cross, the Navy's second-highest decoration, but only Dixon received one. The other two men received commendations for their courage and endurance. As all three had been on the raft together, only Dixon's seniority and leadership can explain the disparity in awards.

AFTERWORD

As the war progressed, vast improvements were made in aircraft navigation. More powerful shipboard and aircraft radars and IFF permitted continuous tracking of aircraft out to one hundred miles or more. In the postwar era, VHF direction finders gave pilots accurate steers to the ship, and TACAN (Tactical Air Navigation system) gave ranges as well as bearings. By 1944 most ships and large aircraft were carrying LORAN (Long-Range Aid to Navigation), an electronic position-fixing device accurate to within a mile. Life rafts and survival equipment were also improved, and a highly efficient Search and Rescue (SAR) system created to recover distressed airmen and seamen quickly.

None of the three men was ever to benefit directly from these great strides in technology, which survival cases such as theirs had helped expedite.

Chief Dixon never flew missions again in combat theaters but spent the remaining years of the war as a ferry pilot, delivering aircraft between factories and repair depots and fleet aviation units. He retired before the end of the war as a lieutenant, having served for a quarter of a century. He lived on his avocado ranch near La Mesa, California, until his wife's failing health forced them to move to San Diego to be near its large Navy medical facility. By odd coincidence, they settled on Albatross Street. After the death of his wife, he married a Navy widow in 1958 and lived in quiet retirement until his death at age eighty-six in 1987. He was buried with military honors in Rosecrans National Cemetery.

Following his epic voyage and promotion to aviation ordnanceman first class, Anthony Pastula was married in 1942 and then served at North Island Naval Air Station (NAS), California, for a year until he was ordered to Pensacola as an instructor in Recognition School. On 16 January 1944, in the late afternoon, his first child was born, exactly two years to the hour after the ditching in the mid-Pacific. Appropriately, the boy was named Gene Anthony, after the two men who had formed a close and enduring friendship following their ordeal on the raft. In April 1945 their friendship was strengthened when Gene Aldrich married Tony's youngest sister, Frances. In June 1945 Tony left the Navy and began work as a Civil Service electronics technician at North Island NAS. He retired in 1973. The next year he made a visit to the museum at the U.S. Naval Academy, where he viewed with considerable emotion the raft on which he and his companions had drifted for so long. It is still a prominent exhibit there.

Three years later Tony and his wife booked passage on Air New Zealand to the Cook Islands, and then on a rusty copra boat to Puka Puka Atoll. The Cook Islands had gained independence from New Zealand in 1965, and the Premier was Sir Albert Henry, the son of the late Resident Agent Geoffrey Henry of Puka Puka, who in 1942 had so generously cared for the shipwrecked sailors. Sir Albert was later succeeded as Premier by his own son, the grandson of Geoffrey Henry. Many of the eight hundred people on the atoll remembered the survivors and welcomed the Pastulas with tears and open arms. It was to both the Americans and the Polynesians a moving moment, and the islanders spared nothing to celebrate the return of their guest of long ago.

Tony Pastula died in 1982, and without military ceremony his ashes were scattered into the Pacific, the sea of his great adventure.

Gene Aldrich served with various aircraft service units during the remaining years of the war and was discharged from the Navy as an aviation chief radioman on 10 December 1946. Like his friend Tony, he then began work as a Civil Service instrument mechanic at North Island NAS. He and his wife, Frances (Tony's sister), had a daughter and two sons, and five grandchildren. In the years after the war, his relationship with his brother-in-law, Tony, was very close, but neither of them had much contact with Lieutenant Dixon. Aldrich, according to relatives, had physical and emotional scars from his ordeal on the raft and died on 27 March 1973 at age fifty-three. He was buried in El Camino Cemetery, San Diego, California, without military ceremonies.

By the end of World War II, many fighting men had passed through harrowing survival situations, usually as a result of enemy actions, culminating in the disastrous sinking of the USS *Indianapolis*, with heavy loss of life, only a few days before the enemy surrendered.

The postwar years brought increasingly sophisticated navigation gear such as satellite, inertial, and Doppler-assisted navigation; sophisticated computers; and now the military Global Positioning System (GPS), accurate within a few feet worldwide and suitable for even small tactical aircraft. Despite such awesome technology, aircraft and ships are still lost through navigation errors or fuel miscalculations, usually human induced. The most advanced computers are no better than the information fed into them.

Survival gear has continued to improve. Inflatable rafts, with integral covers and inflatable floors, and individual survival suits provide protection against both cold and sunburn, and water ballast pockets help prevent capsizing. Compact portable stills use the sun's heat to distill fresh water from sea water, and visual aids for locating survivors have improved too. But today our knowledge of shark behavior is not much greater than that of our early ancestors, and the black dye repellant carried by thousands of aviators during the war was a placebo that made survivors feel safer but did not fool the sharks. Fortunately, shark attacks, though terrifying, are not common.

Perhaps the greatest step forward during the war was the hand-cranked "Gibson Girl" radio, a one-cubic-foot device that sent out distress signals on both low and high frequencies. These signals were detectable hundreds of miles away, and a SAR aircraft could home on them with a direction finder. This device was somewhat cumbersome, and hand-held VHF/UHF radio transceivers, detectable at 20–30 miles, soon followed. These smaller radios permitted homing and two-way conversation between survivors and rescuers. In the past decade, aircraft and earth-circling satellites have been able to receive signals from portable electronic-signal transmitters known as

EPIRBs (Emergency Position Indicating Radio Beacons) and ELTs (Emergency Location Transmitters). These devices provide a fairly accurate distress location and are in widespread use on ships, aircraft, and small pleasure craft. Though these devices have saved several hundred people in recent years, the numerous false alarms generated by carelessness have greatly detracted from their usefulness and resulted in delays of 24–36 hours in responding to genuine distress signals. A new model operating on a dedicated frequency of 406 MHz, capable of worldwide coverage, will have the owner's name and address, type of craft, etc., encoded in the signal and should reduce the false-alarm rate and delay time. These models will be installed in commercial aircraft and ships and will automatically deploy and activate upon impact or sinking.

Despite the advances in navigation and survival gear and the high efficiency of our superb SAR system, numerous other long-term survival cases similar to that of the crew of 6-T-6 have occurred and will likely continue as long as we travel on and over the sea. Many incidents involve people who either cannot afford or refuse to carry adequate survival gear. Some cases follow catastrophic accidents in which the crew is unable to send a distress signal and much of the survival equipment goes down with the craft. This happened to a cruising couple whose boat was rammed repeatedly and sunk by a school of whales 1,200 miles off the Pacific coast of Central America. Despite continuous bumping of their raft by dozens of sharks, the couple was rescued after sixty-six days adrift. In contrast, the crew of a small sailing yacht recently abandoned ship after suffering storm damage. One crew member died in the life raft within hours, while another swam away from the raft after only a day afloat, saying he was going to find some cigarettes!

Long-term survival does not always occur far out at sea. In late 1986 a twenty-seven-year-old native fisherman was on a routine two-hour trip between adjacent cays in the Bahamas when he suffered a steering failure and then fuel exhaustion. Wind and currents swept him out to sea, and he was picked up forty-four days later, sixty miles off Charleston, South Carolina. Though suffering from dehydration and hypothermia, he had survived on raw fish, rain water, and two cans of beer. His first request was for a cold beer! In another case of fuel exhaustion, two young men left Anclote Key, three miles off the Florida mainland, in March 1988. Intense searching for three days in this area of heavy boating did not find them. Two weeks later another boat found them only fifty miles from where they had last been seen. One man had died only two hours before, and the other was semiconscious.

Pitted against the elements with little more than their own ingenuity and will to live, men and women have overcome nearly impossible odds. The example of Dixon, Pastula, and Aldrich, and that of others like them, is a beacon of hope to anyone thrown into a desperate survival situation. Though basic equipment may be missing, the tremendous human resources of mind and heart are still there. They have only to be used.

Robert Trumbull was born in Chicago in 1912 and graduated from the University of Washington at Seattle. He worked as a reporter for the *Honolulu Advertiser* from 1933 to 1943 but began writing for the *New York Times* in 1941, serving as the *Times*'s war correspondent in the Pacific theater until 1945. The U.S. Navy awarded him the Asiatic-Pacific Theater ribbon for his wartime reports. After the war he continued writing for the *Times*, as a foreign correspondent in Japan, the Philippines, South and Southeast Asia 1945–54; as the chief of the Tokyo Bureau 1954–61 and 1964–68; as the chief correspondent in China and Southeast Asia 1961–64; as a correspondent in Australia, New Zealand, and the Pacific islands 1968–73; and as the chief correspondent in Canada 1974–78. Since 1978 he has been a Pacific correspondent, operating out of his home in Honolulu.

Trumbull won the Overseas Press Club award in 1964 for his book *The Scrutable East: A Correspondent's Report on Southeast Asia*. His other books include *Silversides; 100 Best Stories of World War II; India Since Independence; As I See India; Nine Who Survived Hiroshima and Nagasaki; Paradise in Trust; I Can Tell It Now; This Is Communist China;* and *Tin Roofs and Palm Trees: A Report on the New South Seas.* He has also contributed articles on Asian and Pacific affairs to *Encyclopedia Americana, Reader's Digest, Saturday Review,* and *New York Times Magazine.*

John M. Waters, Capt., USCG (Ret.), is an internationally recognized authority on emergency operations, known for his pioneering work in search and rescue and flight safety. From 1964 to 1967 he headed the Coast Guard's Search and Rescue (SAR) Division and then its Aviation Division and developed many of the standard procedures now used in air/sea search and rescue operations. These procedures, set down in two official publications, *National Search and Rescue Manual* and *Aircraft Emergency Procedures over Water,* of which he was the principal author, are the basis for emergency operations followed today by most of the world's commercial airlines and by the U.S. armed forces. He also conceived and obtained funding for the National Search and Rescue School, which trains both U.S. and foreign SAR personnel.

After graduating from the Coast Guard Academy in 1942, Captain Waters saw action in most maritime theaters of World War II and used his experiences in the Battle of the Atlantic to help tell the chilling story of the Allied struggle against deadly German submarines in his book *Bloody Winter,* available from the Naval Institute Press. He served on four ships, two of which he commanded, as well as leading a destroyer escort group. After the war he attended flight school and went on to command two air stations. Captain Waters has participated in more than 5,000 search and rescue missions and is the author most recently of *Rescue at Sea,* also available from the Naval Institute Press.